The 12 Steps
For Adult Children*

*of Alcoholic and other dysfunctional families

The 12 Steps
For Adult Children*

*of Alcoholics and other dysfunctional families

Friends in Recovery

Recovery Publications
1201 Knoxville Street
San Diego, CA 92110
(619) 275-1350

Published by
Recovery Publications
1201 Knoxville Street
San Diego, CA 92110
(619) 275-1350

The Twelve Steps have been reprinted and adapted with permission from Alcoholics Anonymous World Services, Inc. For purposes of this book, the word "alcohol" in Step One has been changed to read "the effects of alcoholism," and the word "alcoholics" in Step Twelve has been changed to read "others."

Printed in the United States of America

Second Printing March 1987
Third Printing April 1987
Fourth Printing August 1987
Fifth Printing October 1987

Recovery Publications

The Twelve Steps For Adult Children.

1.   2.   1.Title
ISBN   0-941405-04-4 $6.95

In memory of Edward, Cecilia,

and the countless others

who never found a solution.

TABLE OF CONTENTS

The 12 Steps
For Adult Children*

*of Alcoholic and other dysfunctional families

AUTHOR'S NOTE

The following characteristics are those most commonly found in Adult Children of Alcoholic and other dysfunctional families. You may find that few or many of these characteristics are present in your life, even though you have no conscious recollection of alcoholism or other dysfuntion in your childhood. These characteristics are referred to in the ACA Program as *THE PROBLEM*. The tenses have been changed to reflect the present. If you identify with any of the traits listed, you will find this book helpful to you from an analytical as well as a spiritual point of view.

1. We are isolated and afraid of authority figures.

2. We are approval seekers and lose our identity in the process.

3. We are frightened by angry people and any personal criticism.

4. We either become alcoholics, marry them, or both—or we find another compulsive personality, such as a workaholic, to fulfill our need for abandonment.

5. We live life from the viewpoint of helping and seeking victims, and we are attracted by the weakness in our love and friendship relationships.

6. We have an overdeveloped sense of responsibility, and it is easier for us to be concerned with others rather than with ourselves. This enables us to avoid looking closely at ourselves.

7. We feel guilty when we stand up for ourselves; instead, we give in to others.

8. We are addicted to excitement.

9. We confuse love with pity and tend to "love" people we can pity and rescue.

10. We stuff back our feelings from our traumatic childhoods and lose the ability to feel or to express our feelings. It hurts so much—(denial).

11. We judge ourselves harshly and have a very low sense of self-esteem, sometimes compensated for by trying to appear superior.

12. We are dependent personalities who are terrified of abandonment. We will do anything to hold on to a relationship in order to avoid experiencing the pain of abandonment. We are conditioned to these types of relationships.

13. Alcoholism is a family disease, and we become para-alcoholics. We take on the characteristics of that disease even though we do not pick up the drink.

14. Para-alcoholics are reactors rather than actors.

INTRODUCTION

As Adult Children of alcoholic or dysfunctional families, we have had to face many difficulties in our lives. The behavior patterns we use today are a direct result of our childhood experiences. Having been raised in homes where conditions were chaotic, we did not learn the proper rules needed to function in a normal manner.

Recognition of this often comes slowly. In order to come to terms with the realities of this condition, we must break many of the old family rules, which include not talking, not trusting, and not feeling. Today, these rules keep us from getting in touch with our true selves.

Behavioral problems in Adult Children are numerous, frequently severe, and sometimes incapacitating. Denial is one of the major problems; it keeps us from the reality of our condition. We tend to behave compulsively and always need to be in control. We have not developed the skills needed to express our feelings, so we keep everything locked inside. Our self-esteem is extremely low, and many of us suffer from severe physical complications.

Adult Children suffer from the disease of co-dependency. This is an emotional, psychological, and behavioral condition that develops from prolonged exposure to a set of unspoken and oppressive rules that prevent us from freely expressing our feelings. Co-dependency affects all persons who are in a relationship with an alcoholic, who have alcoholic relatives, or who grew up in an emotionally repressive family.

Being a victim of alcoholic or other dysfunctional behavior causes pain, fear, and inexpressible rage. These feelings cannot be relieved easily. Consequently, we learn to seek relief through superficial means rather than developing normal ways of feeling secure. We experience temporary "highs" through overachievement, overeating, or misuse of mood-altering substances, such as drugs and alcohol. These "highs" manifest themselves in "all-or-none" functioning. In relationships, our behavior may include pursuing someone who is unavailable to us, and then distancing ourselves. It may include feeling secure one minute, then suddenly fearing abandonment. Or it may include experiencing sensual pleasure and then an unprompted gut-wrenching fear of rejection. These addictive patterns become a way of life, yet we consider ourselves to be normal.

When we finally come to terms with ourselves, we start looking for answers. After exhausting every effort possible, we finally come to the realization that we cannot do it alone. It is at this point that we are ready to accept help. This help can be found in the Twelve Steps, which is a spiritual program of recovery. It is through this spiritual emphasis that we can begin to experience relief from our problems.

The Twelve Steps is not a religious program. Though people using this program find it harmonious with their churches and spiritual beliefs, it has no religious affiliation. It is, however, a program that helps us to discover the spiritual part of ourselves and recognize its importance in our lives. We learn to live our lives according to the guidance of our Higher Power, whatever that may be. We realize that the void or despair we have felt is caused by ignoring or rejecting the spiritual part of ourselves.

The Twelve Step Program can relieve our suffering, fill our emptiness, and help us discover the presence of a power greater than ourselves. This will help us to release great quantities of energy, love, and joy, which are bottled up inside us. It is a loosely structured program that we follow at our own pace, in our own way, with the help of others who are in the Program. All we need is an open mind and a willingness to try. Eventually, our minds will open by themselves with little conscious effort on our part. Most of the work will be done by our unconscious, and we will suddenly notice improvements in ourselves: our awareness, our sensitivity, our ability to love, to be free. We will be surprised by our own spiritual and emotional growth.

The purpose of this book is to help you identify and deal with issues that are interfering with your life. As you work through the problems and rely on the dynamics of the Twelve Steps, you will experience recovery that includes physical, emotional, and spiritual well-being.

Be confident in yourself when studying each step. In this Program, it is important to realize that winners in any field are those who are willing to work and apply themselves in order to succeed. Keeping a positive attitude will be very helpful in your recovery process. Negative thoughts can be very damaging and will slow your progress. Make an effort to surrender to the process, and your negative feelings will be minimized.

There is no right or wrong way to work the Steps. The Twelve Step material that will be used in this book is meant to be suggestive only. We realize we know very little. As we develop a relationship with our Higher Power, more will be disclosed to us. Ask your Higher Power each day what you can do to take better care of yourself. If you have a good relationship with your Higher Power, your life will become less complicated. A commitment to work the Steps as a daily routine for the rest of your life can provide you with the ongoing gift of peace and serenity.

Give freely of what you find and join us. We shall be with you in the Fellowship of Spirit.

GOD BLESS YOU.

STEP ONE

WE ADMITTED WE WERE POWERLESS OVER THE EFFECTS OF ALCOHOLISM— THAT OUR LIVES HAD BECOME UNMANAGEABLE

The idea presented in Step One is overwhelming to most of us until we have begun to see our lives as they really are. It is uncomfortable for us to admit that we are powerless and that our lives are unmanageable. We fight for control and want to keep from being controlled by others. It may be that we are preoccupied with being the smartest or the fastest, or with having the best job. Our obsession may be our status in life, and we find it difficult to believe that we could be powerless. Whatever we do, and however it may be labeled, some of our behavior involves doing things that are against our better judgement. Step One places us on the threshold of identifying the root cause of behavior over which we have no control and which we seem unable to stop.

Prior to becoming aware of our problem, we try everything possible to "fix" things. We know that something is wrong and that our life is not working. No matter what we do or where we look, things get progressively worse. We may suffer anxiety attacks or uncontrollable compulsive behavior. When we actually come to grips with ourselves and realize that we need help, we are ready for Step One. We have no alternative but to admit that we are powerless, and that our lives have become unmanageable.

1

Step One is the foundation for all the Steps. When working this Step, we see the facts of our lives in true perspective. It is not the purpose of this Step to judge ourselves. It is an opportunity to observe our behavior and to admit that we need help. When we surrender to this idea, we will see our behavior as it really is and be willing to be honest with ourselves. It is through this honesty that we begin to achieve serenity.

Step One consists of two distinct parts: (1) The admission that we have an obsessive desire to control and that we are experiencing the effects of an addictive process that has rendered us powerless over our own behavior; and (2) The admission that our lives have been, are now, and will continue to be unmanageable by us alone.

Admitting our powerlessness over the effects of alcoholism or other addictive behavior is what brings us to the ACA Program. Here we can begin a process of recovery that will transform our lives. Since dysfunctional behavior is a major characteristic of our disease, we must realize that our mind, with its acquired traits, habits, and character defects, has caused us to become powerless over our behavior. By recalling our childhood histories, we see that, years before we realized it, we were out of control. Our obsessions even then were not a habit but indeed the beginning of a fatal progressive disease.

Our instinct cries out against the idea of personal powerlessness and the fact that we are not in control. We have been accustomed to accepting full responsibility for all that happens in our lives as well as in the lives of others. This contradicts the idea that we are powerless. How can we be fully responsible and at the same time be powerless? Until we hit bottom through utter defeat, we will be unable to take the first step toward liberation and renewed strength. The fact that we are powerless is a truth we must realize before we can totally surrender.

Admitting that our lives are unmanageable is equally as difficult as admitting that we are powerless. We see ourselves as responsible adults, holding a job, managing a house, and performing the required tasks on a daily basis. We have been taught from childhood that the best way to succeed is to manage our lives effectively. We were told that truly successful people manage their own lives as well as the lives of others.

In order to come to terms with the fact that our lives are unmanageable, we need to recognize that managing our lives is impossible. As we reflect on our lives, we can conclude that no matter what we were doing to manage our lives, the results were never quite what we planned. When we take time to realize that our depressions and frustrations are signs that we are not doing as good a job as we think we are doing, we begin to see the unmanageability. We see how we rationalize our behavior and make excuses for ourselves, blaming our action on fatigue, stress, or other people. Once we can look at our lives objectively and recognize our own faults, we drop our disguise and become more honest with ourselves. We see that our lives are unmanageable and not at all what we would like them to be.

Though the First Step may seem overwhelming, it merely points out our human limitations, which have so long been a source of discomfort to us. For most of our lives, we have tried to hide from ourselves. This has prevented us from facing the reality of our situation. Step One is the first step toward the humility we need to find spiritual guidance through reliance on a Higher Power.

In the process of accepting our powerlessness and unmanageability, we must be willing to put aside the false pride that nearly killed us. Although working Step One can be painful for us, the road to recovery begins with surrender. Until we accept this truth, our progress toward recovery will be hindered. Although it is difficult for many of us to accept this fact, we must realize that we cannot manage our own lives or control our thinking. Our healing begins when we are willing to acknowledge our problem. This first step forms the foundation for working each of the Twelve Steps.

STEP TWO

CAME TO BELIEVE THAT A POWER GREATER THAN OURSELVES COULD RESTORE US TO SANITY

Acceptance of our powerlessness leads us naturally into Step Two. By this time, we have begun to see the results of our past beliefs. "Came to believe" implies a former non-belief, or living life with other beliefs. The result of this lifestyle is our powerlessness and unmanageability. For some of us, belief in our self-will was all we had. Belief in a Higher Power did not seem necessary. Until we took Step One and admitted our powerlessness and unmanageability, we were operating on self-will alone. We simply did not entertain the idea of a Higher Power. As we begin to accept the notion of a Power greater than ourselves, we start to function in a healthier way. We begin to feel a sense of peace and serenity that we had never felt before. We recognize that we are human beings who are struggling to survive with certain limitations.

Step Two is referred to as the Hope Step. It is the springboard from which we begin the journey toward spiritual awakening. In Step One, we felt hopeless and beaten as we surrendered. Step Two gives us new hope as we begin to see that there is help available if we simply come to believe. We no longer need to struggle alone. It is our chance to end our old patterns of behavior and emerge into a new lifestyle. Our deep desire is to become the person we were meant to be.

Step Two provides us with the foundation for the spiritual growth we seek in order to achieve our fulfillment.

Newcomers often find two major problems with this Step. The first is a belief in a Power greater than ourselves. We may have heard or read that "faith as small as a mustard seed can work wonders." If doubt persists, we may be denying the idea of a Higher Power's healing presence. We might find it impossible to imagine that even a Higher Power could heal our obsessions and compulsions. By accepting the fact that the most devout spiritual seekers suffer from dark moments of doubt, our faith can be strengthened. Our willingness to believe and to ask to have our faith strengthened marks the beginning of our spiritual development. This is the foundation of the ACA Twelve Step Program. The second problem with this step is the implication of insanity. Having recognized that our lives are unmanageable, we must come to terms with the fact that we need a new director. These are powerful issues and, at first, can be frightening. For many of us, they are definite contradictions of our old beliefs and lifestyle.

Before entering the Program, many of us move away from the idea of anything spiritual. We don't understand it, or don't like the idea of it. Our lack of trust in others sometimes blocks our ability to accept the fact that there could be a spiritual being who could offer us support. The basis for these beliefs may lie in the fact that we have become accustomed to having our self-will dictate every action. We are self-sufficient and don't see a need for outside support. Our prayers may not have been answered, and we may have lost confidence in a Higher Power. It is possible that our self-esteem is so low that we do not feel worthy of a Higher Power. We believe that we need to do everything ourselves, and we don't trust anyone.

If we have been successful in completing Step One, we have a good foundation for accepting the concept of a Higher Power. Having surrendered our powerlessness in Step One, we have become aware that our self-will has been getting in our way. When we discover there is a Power greater than ourselves, we let go of our self-will and can find our own God.

Many people have found that all that is required to "come to believe" is to attend meetings on a regular basis. Through the dynamics of the Program, it becomes obvious that something is working for the people at the meetings. If we are willing to keep an open mind and recognize the success that people are enjoying, the rest can happen easily.

Our willingness to surrender and to believe in the process helps us to replace our self-will and allows our unconscious to take over. When this happens, the idea of a Higher Power becomes acceptable to us. We shift our attention away from wanting our addictive behavior to change, and we begin to understand that life is a process. Working the Steps and being healed is a process. This shift of focus reveals the presence of a Higher Power assisting, empowering, and doing things for us that we could not possibly have managed ourselves.

During the beginning stages of accepting the presence of a Higher Power, it is sometimes helpful to make a game of it. We can look on chance events and coincidences in our lives as being miracles, or gifts, from our Higher Power. By taking time to thank our Higher Power for simple things, like "not getting a ticket for running a red light" or "finding a beautiful dress on sale," we can learn to accept and appreciate His presence in our lives. This may seem silly at first, but it helps us to "come to believe."

Step Two does not mean that we must immediately come to believe in God as He may be presented in various religious denominations. In fact, our belief in God may come only as a result of seeing His power at work in our lives. All that is required is a willingness to believe there is a Power greater than ourselves. This Power can be whatever we choose it to be. It can be God as we understand Him, a friend, a partner, a person from the Program, or the Program itself. For some of us, God can be Love.

Belief in a Power greater than ourselves is central to becoming the happy, positive, and loving person we are truly meant to be. Inasmuch as our old ways led us into the depths of despair, we became self-centered, lonely, and detached from ourselves. We found that our reasoning mind could not solve all our problems.

Step Two implies that we are insane. The dictionary defines insanity as "inability to manage one's own affairs and perform one's social duties" and "without recognition of one's own illness." If this is our first exposure to the Steps, we may not be totally aware of the extent of our illness. We may still be blaming outside circumstances for our condition rather than admitting responsibility for our own behavior.

Many of us have acquired certain characteristics and personality traits that protect us from the realities of life. Some of the more common characteristics are being defiant, self-sufficient, indifferent, resentful, self-deluded, and self-centered. These alone are an indication that we suffer from some form of insanity—that we behave insanely in many areas of our lives.

In order to make changes in our lives, we must be willing to look at ourselves honestly and recognize our own degree of insanity. It is easy for the alcoholic or chemically dependent person to accept his insanity, because his addictive behavior is obviously insane. For adult children, it is more difficult to accept insanity because we are not aware of our behavior. It is easy for us to deceive ourselves and look to outside sources for the cause of our dysfunction. We have a degree of responsibility in being aware of people, places, and things that activate our insane behavior. When we break through this self-delusion, we become ready to accept our behavior as being insane in many cases.

As we come in contact with others and listen to their stories, we are exposed to experiences similar to ours. It becomes clear to us that we each maintain "emotional sobriety" only one day at a time and that we are in remission rather than totally cured. We must continually work at improving the quality of our lives. We eventually come to the realization that anything we do or think that is destructive to ourselves or to someone else is insane. Based on this, worry is insane, as well as depressions, compulsions, and obsessions. The mere fact that we believe we can control others is insane.

Our society as a whole is insane. We are taught from youth to do what is right, and it is expected that we know the difference between right and wrong. Based on our role models, the message as to what is right and wrong is not always clear. It is expected that we conduct ourselves responsibly and are able to manage our own lives. Since we cannot manage our own lives, it must be concluded that we do not know the difference between right and wrong. When we can accept this, we are truly ready to admit that we behave insanely.

When we started this program, we may have been expecting instant results. During our childhood, it may have been common to see anger or confusion when things didn't happen "right now." In this program sudden change is the exception, not the rule. It requires patience and understanding to achieve the recovery we are looking for. Each of us is unique, and recovery begins for us at different stages in the Steps. Some of us may experience instant relief, whereas others may not begin to feel different until later in the Steps.

Coming to believe in a Higher Power and admitting our insanity require a great deal of humility. Lack of humility is what got us to the position we are in today, and it is important to practice humility in all our affairs. Humility is a recurrent theme of the Program, and our growth is enhanced by our willingness to be humble. As we attend meetings and work the Steps, we discover a peace and serenity that is possible only through our surrender and the desire to improve the quality of our lives.

When we become ready to accept fully our powerlessness and unmanageability (Step One), when we accept a Higher Power and our insanity (Step Two), we will be ready to take action and turn our lives over to the care of God as we understand Him (Step Three). There is no need to hurry. The important thing is that we are ready and that we have the faith necessary to proceed with the remaining Steps.

STEP THREE

MADE A DECISION TO TURN OUR WILL AND OUR LIVES OVER TO THE CARE OF GOD AS WE UNDERSTOOD HIM

Step Three requires that we take affirmative action as a result of the developing awareness we have gained from working the first two steps. In Step One, we admitted we were powerless, that our lives had become unmanageable. In Step Two, we came to believe that a Power greater than ourselves could restore us to sanity.

Step Three seems to require more of us than the first two steps because we are now asked to turn ourselves over to a Higher Power with total abandon. If we feel pressured by this decision, we are going too fast. We must slow down and take the time needed to become ready to proceed. It is in these first three steps that we set the foundation for working all of the steps and for achieving the peace and serenity we are looking for.

The key to success in working Step Three lies in our willingness to turn our lives over to the care of God. This is difficult for many of us because we are so accustomed to handling our lives on self-will alone. Our self-will has barred God from our lives, and the idea of surrender is frightening. We learned to pray to God and to ask Him for things we want, but we were always in control. We are accustomed to asking Him for guidance in helping us achieve our goals. This is different from turning our very essence over to Him to do whatever He wants without our having any say in the matter.

If we have successfully worked Steps One and Two, we have accepted our situation and are ready to look for a new manager of our lives. Letting our Higher Power guide our lives becomes a little easier when we realize that we haven't done such a good job so far. Our fears and resentments become manageable when we choose God as our new director. We discover that we can impact our lives in a positive way. As we begin to rely on a Higher Power, we become willing to turn our lives over and to trust in the results.

In the beginning stages of turning our lives over, we will possibly experience resistance. This may be attributed to our need for independence since most of us thrive on being in charge and cling to the illusion of being free to "do our own thing." We may concede only the problems that are causing us the most pain. This is usually a start, and will provide us with the confidence needed as we see that God has answers to all of our problems. As we become more comfortable with the fact that our problems do diminish, we become more willing to accept the notion of turning our entire lives over to His care.

Experience tells us that the more willing we are, the faster the Program will come to us, the faster we will get its meaning and be able to live it. If we try too hard consciously, we will become impatient and block our progress with frustration, irritation, resentment, and self-pity.

The central theme of Step Three is best expressed by the slogan "Let Go and Let God." The idea of letting go can help us greatly because we see that surrendering our will only allows for our further growth. We begin to realize that God takes good care of us. As long as we do the "footwork" and do not expect God to do everything for us, we will find God's will for us and be able to carry out His plan.

Our thinking mind, using instinct and logic to bolster our ego, tells us that we will become nothing if we turn our will and our lives over to the care of God. Strange as it may seem, the more we are willing to depend on a Higher Power, the more independent we become. Our dependence on God is actually a means of gaining the true spiritual independence that we all seek.

Caution is an important factor in completing this Step. If we are not completely comfortable with the idea of turning our will and our lives over to the care of God, we must slow down and do more work. Some of us may still be experiencing the powerful impact of our addictive behavior. Whatever it involves, be it relationships, money, drugs, or food, we face the prospect of spiritual as well as physical death. We began this program because the path we were on was destroying our life. This behavior was a way to temporarily numb the emotional pain, distract our boredom, or relieve us of stress. Being asked to trust in a Higher Power may present a challenge to us since we in no way can manipulate or manage God.

The Twelve Steps is a spiritual program. Step Three is an opportunity to let a Spiritual Power greater than us take charge of the rest of our lives. Fundamentally, this also means we may stop feeling responsible for everything and everybody. This is simply to say that the way to experience peace and serenity is to surrender.

It is not important to understand a Higher Power in order to let go. We need only believe in the process for our own well-being. If we are having trouble taking Step Three, it is probably because we did not successfully take Step Two. In this case, it is important to return to Step Two before proceeding.

Once we are ready to take Step Three, we will see a change come over us. We will appear calmer and feel that a weight has been lifted from our shoulders. It can happen right away or gradually over a day or two as our consciousness begins to recognize that a Higher Power seems to be taking over. Don't expect to remain in this state of euphoria forever. There will be times when we take our wills back, and we need only to recognize this. There are no saints in this Program; we will have slips. However, as we continue to work the Program on a daily basis, we will see that we become more ready and willing to continually turn our lives over.

There is a paradox in the way this program seems to work. When we give up managing our own lives and begin to trust in God's will for us, we will find we are calmer and more accepting of things around us. Friends will compliment us on how well we are managing our lives. As we stop trying to keep ourselves on a straight and narrow path of self-discipline, people will begin to recognize how well-disciplined we are.

Most of us who start this Program do so in search of answers to the complex questions of life and also to find a way to stop repeating painful cycles of ineffective behavior. In the past, some of us may have experimented with lifestyles and beliefs that appeared to present solutions. What we are really looking for is a personal experience of God that transcends the arguments over mankind's conflicting dogmas.

If you are prepared to take Step Three, repeat the step out loud right now. Follow your assertion of the Third Step with the AA Third Step Prayer. This prayer is a powerful way to focus your daily intention to turn your life over to the care of God.

THIRD STEP PRAYER

"God, I offer myself to Thee—to build with me and do with me as Thou wilt. Relieve me of the bondage of self, that I may better do Thy will. Take away my difficulties, that victory over them may bear witness to those I would help of Thy Power, Thy Love, and Thy Way of Life. May I do Thy Will always."[1]

THIRD STEP GIFT

Striving for recognition . . .
An appearance of superiority . . .
Accomplishment . . .
A relationship that fits my picture.

All a mirage, relentless
Thirsting to fill the emptiness within . . .
Incessently demanding more
and more.

Yet - ever present, within,
Serene and uncritical . . .
Poised in the gentle stillness
of infinite patience . . .
Spirit . . .
My Higher Power . . .
Comforting Love . . .
Awaits.

1. Alcoholics Anonymous, Alcoholics Anonymous World Services, Inc., (New York), p.63.

STEP FOUR

MADE A SEARCHING AND FEARLESS MORAL INVENTORY OF OURSELVES

Our introduction to the ACA Program occurs as a result of a series of very painful events brought about by the external pressures of reality. The pain of this reality has weakened the defenses that comprise our denial system, and we are forced to look at ourselves and see the consequences of our addictive behavior. Our shock and our acknowledgment of the serious problems in our lives form the beginning of an adventure in self-discovery and recovery. We start facing ourselves and uncovering our acquired character defects. When we accept the fact that these character defects are acquired, we can come to terms with how they have controlled us in the past, and then we can let go of them.

As part of this process, we become aware of the denial that has protected us from the reality of our addictive behavior and preserved our limited sense of self-worth and dignity. Step Four will help us to deal with our denial system which has been one of our major survival techniques. Denial has distorted our perception and impaired our judgment so that we have become self-deluded and incapable of accurate self-awareness.

Denial is the core component of our illness. To a greater or lesser extent, it can be found in all of us. It can be the fatal aspect of our illness because it keeps us locked into an

17

increasingly destructive pattern. It consists of many defenses and maneuvers that we use to protect ourselves from the reality of our condition. Step Four is a helpful tool for penetrating our denial system, and it provides us with an opportunity to learn a great deal about our illness and its consequences. Denial is seen in many different forms and operates in various ways, some of which are as follows:

1. Pretending that something does not exist when in reality it does.
2. Being willing to admit there is a problem but unwilling to see the severity of it.
3. Seeing the problem as being caused by something or someone else. The behavior is not denied, but its cause is someone else's responsibility.
4. Offering excuses, alibis, justifications, and other explanations for behavior.
5. Dealing with the problem on a general level, avoiding personal and emotional awareness of the situation or conditions.
6. Changing the subject to avoid threatening topics.
7. Becoming angry and irritable when reference is made to the condition. This helps to avoid the issue.

During the first three steps, we faced many changes in our lives. In Step One, we admitted that we were powerless, that our lives had become unmanageable. In Step Two, we came to believe in a Higher Power as a means of restoring our sanity. In Step Three, we made a decision to turn our will and our lives over to the care of God as we understood Him.

An inventory is not a history. It relates to what is on hand at the moment. It is a list of things in stock now and does not concern what was there in the past. Looking at the inventory this way, it is easier to make it a fearless inventory because we have no reason to fear the present. Writing is important and is a key to success in working Step Four. As we list our qualities, we will discover both good and bad traits that will amaze us. It is important not to judge ourselves but rather to recognize that our main goal is to accept what we discover.

As we more completely understand the childhood origin of much of our behavior, we will develop a mature perspective on our being adult children. Understanding our behavior is only part of the task we are faced with in reaching our inner child. We have no doubt identified some of our childhood behaviors, and we understand them to be dysfunctional. However, we continue to repeat them unconsciously and are frustrated by their reappearance. This can be likened to gardeners continually lopping off tops of weeds that, just as persistently, regrow from the roots. They didn't seem to comprehend the whole job, which was to get to the roots that lay hidden beneath the surface. Step Four uncovers many childhood roots that can be dealt with through the help of our Higher Power. This process is a vital key to our personal transformation.

Two of the linkpins that hold our problem behavior in place are resentment and fear. They have had a strong impact on our childhood, and we still find them deeply influencing our adult behavior. Resentment, among other feelings of unexpressed anger, is thought to be the source from which many mental and physical ills originate. Going through life with deep resentments can only result in futility and unhappiness. If we allow our resentments (fancied or real) to dominate us, they have the power to destroy us.

The destructive power of fear is equally detrimental and corrosive to the fabric of our lives. At this point in our recovery, we may find fear in all our behaviors. Whatever its origin, given a particular situation in our daily lives (e.g. is fear of abandonment or authority figures), fear will set in motion a sequence of circumstances that will bring about a misfortune we feel we don't deserve. As we inventory our fears, we may find that their presence is particularly evident when our self-reliance fails us. Our belief may be that if we only had enough self-confidence, we wouldn't have this problem. Here, again, our self-delusion is dangerous. If we have sincerely taken Step Three, we are now prepared to trust and rely upon an infinite God instead of our finite selves.

Being willing to face our resentments and fears takes courage. However, our faith in our Higher Power is the tap root through which we will let Him demonstrate what He can do. The spiritual sickness that is tied to resentment and fear is the malady we can overcome by sincerely working these Steps with our Higher Power. Having a spiritual healing will straighten out the crippling mental and physical conditions of our lives.

Step Four provides a means for viewing ourselves honestly, possibly for the first time. This can be the beginning of a new awareness of ourselves. Some of the discoveries may be overwhelming to us. In that case, we need only turn the responsibility for acceptance of ourselves over to our Higher Power. If we have successfully worked Steps One through Three, this should be relatively easy.

As we prepare our Fourth Step inventory, we will be looking at our character traits and seeing our strengths and weaknesses. Our strengths are seen in behavior that has positive effects on ourselves as well as on others. Our weaknesses manifest themselves in behavior that is destructive to ourselves and to others. Before we can correct our problem areas, we need to examine and acknowledge our weaknesses. This understanding lies in discovering how we talk to ourselves— the ideas, beliefs, and attitudes that govern how we act.

The inventory you will be preparing is for your own benefit. It can be a tool for making a major breakthrough in your recovery and for setting you on the road to freedom. As you write the inventory, certain feelings may arise. If you notice that you are having difficulty being completely honest, denial may still be at work. Stop for a moment and reflect on what your true feelings are. Take time to "tune in" to your true feelings so that you can rid yourself of the excess baggage you have been carrying for an indefinite period of time. Remember that your Higher Power is with you and is prepared to offer the support and guidance you need to complete this work.

The material offered in this Fourth Step Inventory Guide is somewhat different from the inventory guides used in other Twelve Step Programs. The emphasis is on the character defects most commonly seen in adult children. When preparing the inventory, choose behavior traits that specifically apply to you. Use recent events and record words and actions as accurately as possible.

List specific examples of your behavior, including WHO, WHEN, WHERE, WHAT. As part of being specific, give the names of all persons involved in the situation with you (WHO). Record the date this behavior took place (WHEN). Indicate where this behavior took place (WHERE). Finally, describe your behavior and tell what you did (WHAT).

RESENTMENT AND FEAR EXERCISE

Resentment and fear are the major sources of all forms of spiritual disease. Our mental and physical ills are the result of this unwholesome condition. Learning to deal with resentment and fear is an important part of our recovery process.

Examine situations in which resentment or fear is a problem for you. Answer the following questions when describing these conditions.

a. What or who do you resent or fear? (people, institutions, principles)

b. Why are you resentful or afraid? (What happened to cause this?)

c. How has this resentment or fear affected you? (e.g. self-esteem, finances, goals, relationships, sex, physical harm or threats)

EXAMPLES: (a) I RESENT my boss (b) BECAUSE he doesn't care to hear my story about why I am depressed. (c) THIS AFFECTS my self-esteem.

(a) I FEAR my spouse (b) BECAUSE I can never please him. (c) THIS AFFECTS my self-esteem and sexuality.

CHARACTER TRAITS

Below is an example to assist you in completing your inventory.

ISOLATION

1. List examples of your behavior that indicate you are isolating yourself.

    I often turn down invitations to go to parties.
    I am bashful at work and am afraid to express my feelings or ask for help.

2. What do you believe is the underlying cause of this behavior? (e.g. fear, resentment, anger, guilt)

    I fear that people will judge me because I am unattractive, and I don't usually socialize. I remember being criticized by my parents for the way I behaved because I was so quiet.

3. What is being hurt, threatened, or interfered with? (e.g. self-esteem, goals, security, personal or sexual relations)

    I feel my self-esteem is hurt when I expose myself to others, and I judge myself without mercy. This interferes with my desire to have a relationship and meet new people.

RECOVERY FROM ISOLATION

1. List examples that indicate you isolate yourself less frequently.

    In feeling more comfortable at social gatherings, I've noticed that I can easily engage in conversation and that I have interesting things to contribute. I have been able to share with friends my discomfort about getting together for activities. I also feel good about the risks I take when I share my feelings, and I recognize that my friends accept where I am.

2. What do you hope to achieve as you become more confident about situations from which you would usually isolate yourself?

    I want to cultivate new, healthy relationships in which sharing feelings honestly is okay. I hope to become more assertive so that I can achieve more success in my career.

ANGER

DESCRIPTION

Anger is a major source of many of our problems. It is a feeling that we often suppress because it is so uncomfortable for us. In our chaotic homes, the turmoil was so intense that we learned to deny our anger. We felt safer not expressing our anger and hoped it would go away. We eventually became unaware of its presence. Repressed anger leads to serious resentment and depression. It causes physical complications, which lead to stress-related illnesses. Denying anger causes problems in relationships because we are not being truthful about our feelings. We are fearful of alienating people and destroying relationships.

FEELINGS AND BEHAVIOR

1. RESENTMENT
2. SELF-PITY
3. JEALOUSY
4. PREJUDICE

5. DEPRESSION
6. SADNESS
7. PHYSICAL ILLNESS

RECOVERY FROM ANGER

DESCRIPTION

Learning to express anger is a major step toward recovery. It releases us from a lot of hidden emotions and allows healing to take place. Expressing anger is a vehicle for setting boundaries and helps us to be honest with ourselves. As we become willing to express anger honestly, we find that we move beyond the emotion and that we are better able to cope with the situation. Our relationships improve as we begin to feel safe in expressing ourselves. Stress-related problems diminish, and we feel better physically.

FEELINGS AND BEHAVIOR

1. EXPRESS ANGER
2. IDENTIFY TRUE
   FEELINGS

3. SET BOUNDARIES
4. INNER CALM AND PEACE

APPROVAL SEEKING

DESCRIPTION

As a result of our dysfunctional upbringing, we fear disapproval and criticism. What we wanted so desperately as children was to receive approval from our parents, grandparents, siblings, and significant others. This occurred rarely for most of us, so we were constantly seeking validation of ourselves. The need for validation continues into adulthood and manifests itself in the way we pattern our behavior around the desires of others. This behavior keeps us out of touch with our true feelings and causes us to be insecure. It prevents us from discovering our own wants and needs. We are always on the lookout for others' reactions and attempt to manage their impressions of us. We constantly please everyone and remain loyal to extremes.

FEELINGS AND BEHAVIOR

1. ABANDONMENT OF SELF
2. DISHONESTY
3. IMPRESSION MANAGEMENT
4. FEAR OF FAILURE
5. EXTREME LOYALTY
6. PEOPLE PLEASING
7. FEAR OF PERSONAL CRITICISM
8. IGNORING OUR OWN NEEDS
9. INSECURITY (LACK OF CONFIDENCE)

RECOVERY FROM APPROVAL SEEKING

DESCRIPTION

We begin to rely on our own approval and on that of our Higher Power. We understand that wanting approval is okay, but we no longer need to seek approval, or validation, from outside sources. We accept compliments from others and learn to simply say thank you, believing that the compliment is sincere. We say yes when it feels comfortable, and we are willing to say no when it doesn't feel right.

FEELINGS AND BEHAVIOR

1. RECOGNIZE OUR OWN NEEDS
2. TELL THE TRUTH ABOUT HOW WE FEEL
3. SELF-LOYALTY
4. SECURITY IN BEING OURSELVES

CARETAKING

DESCRIPTION

As long as we take care of others, solve their problems, and supply their needs, we are not required to look at ourselves. As this trait becomes more pronounced, we lose our own identity. As children, we took on the concerns and problems of others far beyond our years and, in many cases, were deprived of a normal childhood. The attention we got caused us to believe we had God-like powers. Taking care of others boosted our self-esteem and made us feel indispensable. It gave purpose to our life. As caretakers, we are most comfortable with chaotic situations in which we can be reassured that we are needed. We often end up as martyrs and never experience the joy of taking care of ourselves.

FEELINGS AND BEHAVIOR

1. HELP AND SEEK "VICTIMS"
2. RESCUE PEOPLE
3. IGNORE OUR NEEDS
4. SUPER-RESPONSIBLE
5. MAKE OURSELVES INDISPENSABLE
6. LOSS OF IDENTITY

RECOVERY FROM CARETAKING

DESCRIPTION

As we leave the role of caretaker, we stop being responsible for everyone and allow each individual to find his own way. We understand that everyone has a Higher Power, which is the best source for guidance, love, and support. We become free from the burden of meeting everyone's needs and find time to develop our own personalities. Our obsession to care for others is replaced with the acceptance that we are powerless over the lives of others and that our only responsibility in life is for our own welfare and happiness.

FEELINGS AND BEHAVIOR

1. STOP RESCUING
2. CARE FOR OURSELVES
3. SET BOUNDARIES
4. DETACH FROM "VICTIM" RELATIONSHIPS

CONTROL

DESCRIPTION

As children, we had little control over our environment or the events that took place in our lives. As adults, we control our feelings and behavior, and we try to control the feelings and behavior of others. We become rigid, manipulative, and we lack spontaneity in our lives. There is an element of distrust in our need to control. We trust only ourselves to carry out a task or to handle a situation. We manipulate others in order to manage their impressions of us, and we keep a balance that feels safe for us. We fear that our lives will get worse if we let go of control. We become stressed and anxious when control is not possible.

FEELINGS AND BEHAVIOR

1. OVERREACTION TO CHANGE
2. RIGIDITY
3. INTOLERANCE
4. FEAR OF FAILURE
5. JUDGMENTALISM
6. LACK OF TRUST
7. DIFFICULTY HAVING FUN
8. MANIPULATION OF OTHERS

RECOVERY FROM CONTROL

DESCRIPTION

As we become more aware of our controlling behavior, we realize that we are powerless and that we have no control over anything or anyone except ourselves. We stop manipulating situations in an effort to get our way, and we begin accepting our Higher Power as the ultimate source of security. As we begin to surrender our will and our lives to the care of God, we eliminate a great deal of stress and anxiety. We become willing to participate without being concerned about the outcome. Recital of the Serenity Prayer can be a helpful tool in correcting our desire to control.

FEELINGS AND BEHAVIOR

1. ACCEPTANCE OF CHANGE
2. TRUST IN PEOPLE
3. LET GO
4. REDUCE STRESS LEVELS
5. LEARN TO HAVE FUN
6. ACCEPT OTHERS AS THEY ARE

FEAR OF ABANDONMENT

DESCRIPTION

As children, we observed unpredictable behavior. Never knowing from one day to the next whether our parents would be there, many of us were abandoned either physically or emotionally. Fear of abandonment was a pattern established in early childhood because of our desperate attempts to please our parents. However, as their addiction increased in severity, we simply did not exist. As adults, we choose partners with whom we can re-enact this fear. By trying hard to be perfect and to meet our partner's needs, we avoid conflicts in order to avoid experiencing the pain of our past. Reducing this pain takes precedence over dealing with the issues, or conflicts, and creates an environment of tension and poor communication.

FEELINGS AND BEHAVIOR

1. INSECURITY
2. CARETAKING
3. WORRY
4. FEELING GUILTY WHEN STANDING UP FOR OURSELVES

RECOVERY FROM FEAR OF ABANDONMENT

DESCRIPTION

By relying upon the ever-present love of our Higher Power, our self-worth increases; our fear of, and need for, abandonment diminishes. We seek out healthy relationships with people who love and take care of themselves. We feel more secure in revealing our feelings. We transfer our old dependence on others to our Higher Power. We learn to understand and accept a nurturing and loving fellowship in ACA. Our self-confidence grows as we begin to realize that we will never again be totally alone.

FEELINGS AND BEHAVIOR

1. TRUE EXPRESSIONS OF FEELINGS
2. SELF-CONFIDENCE
3. CONSIDER OUR OWN NEEDS IN A RELATIONSHIP
4. REDUCE OUR CARETAKING

27

FEAR OF PEOPLE AND AUTHORITY FIGURES

DESCRIPTION

Unwarranted fear of people in roles of authority is a result of low self-esteem. We are unable to deal with people whom we perceive as being in a position of power. Common assertiveness displayed by people is often misinterpreted by us as anger. This can cause us to feel intimidated and to become oversensitive. No matter how competent we are, we compare ourselves to others and often conclude that we are inadequate. As a result, we accept compromise and avoid confrontation or criticism.

FEELINGS AND BEHAVIOR

1. FEAR OF REJECTION
2. OVERSENSITIVITY
3. SELF-ESTEEM (PRIDE)
4. COMPARING
5. REACT RATHER THAN ACT
6. INADEQUACY

RECOVERY FROM FEAR OF PEOPLE
AND AUTHORITY FIGURES

DESCRIPTION

As we begin to feel comfortable and involved with people and authority figures, we stop focusing on pleasing and begin to behave as our true selves. We then recognize everyone as being like us, with their own fears, defenses, and insecurities. Others' behavior (assertiveness, etc.) no longer dictates how we feel about ourselves. We start acting rather than reacting when responding to others. We recognize that our ultimate authority figure is our Higher Power, who is always with us.

FEELINGS AND BEHAVIOR

1. INCREASED SELF-ESTEEM
2. STAND UP FOR OURSELVES
3. ACCEPT POSITIVE CRITICISM
4. INTERACT WITH PEOPLE AND AUTHORITY FIGURES

FROZEN FEELINGS

DESCRIPTION

Many of us have difficulty expressing feelings or even realizing that we have feelings. We harbor deep emotional pain and a deeply felt sense of guilt. As children, our feelings were met with disapproval, anger, and rejection. As a means of survival, we learned to hide our feelings or repress them entirely. As adults, we are not in touch with our feelings. We can only experience "acceptable" feelings in order to be safe. Feelings are distorted so that we can protect ourselves from reality. Distorted and repressed feelings cause resentment, anger, and depression, which eventually lead to physical illness.

FEELINGS AND BEHAVIOR

1. OUT OF TOUCH WITH FEELINGS
2. DISTORTED FEELINGS
3. SUPPRESSED FEELINGS
4. AVOIDANCE OF FEELINGS
5. PHYSICAL ILLNESS

RECOVERY FROM FROZEN FEELINGS

DESCRIPTION

As we get in touch with our feelings and learn to express them, wonderful things begin to happen. Our stress levels decrease, and we begin to see ourselves as worthwhile people. We learn that expression of feelings is a great way to communicate, and we find that our needs can be met. All we have to do is ask. As we begin to release our feelings, we experience some levels of pain. But the pain goes away, and we develop a sense of peace and serenity. The more willing we are to take risks in releasing our emotions, the more effective our recovery will be.

FEELINGS AND BEHAVIOR

1. FACING REALITY
2. OPEN EXPRESSION OF FEELINGS
3. ABILITY TO CRY
4. EXPRESS NEEDS TO OTHERS

ISOLATION

DESCRIPTION

We find it safe in many instances to detach ourselves from surroundings that are uncomfortable to us. By isolating ourselves, we are preventing others from seeing us as we really are. We tell ourselves that we are not worthy and, therefore, do not deserve anything. We also tell ourselves that we cannot be punished or hurt if we don't express our feelings. Rather than take risks, we choose to procrastinate, thereby eliminating the need to face an uncertain outcome.

FEELINGS AND BEHAVIOR

1. FEAR OF REJECTION
2. FEEL DIFFERENT FROM OTHERS
3. NON-ASSERTIVENESS
4. DEFEATISM
5. LONELINESS
6. PROCRASTINATION

RECOVERY FROM ISOLATION

DESCRIPTION

As we begin to feel better about ourselves, we become willing to take risks and to expose ourselves to new surroundings. We seek out friends and relationships that are nurturing, safe, and supportive. We learn to participate and to have fun in group activities. It becomes easier to express our feelings as we develop a higher sense of self-esteem. We recognize that people will accept us for who we really are. Our self-acceptance allows us to experience the precious gift of life.

FEELINGS AND BEHAVIOR

1. SELF-ACCEPTANCE
2. FREE EXPRESSION OF EMOTION
3. CULTIVATE MUTUALLY SUPPORTIVE RELATIONSHIPS
4. COMPLETE PROJECTS
5. ACTIVE PARTICIPATION IN FUNCTIONS

LOW SELF-ESTEEM

DESCRIPTION

Low self-esteem is rooted in our early childhood, during which we never felt quite adequate. As a result of constant criticism, we believed that we were bad and that we were the cause of many of the family problems. In order to feel accepted, we tried harder to please. The harder we tried, the more frustrated we became. Low self-esteem affects our ability to set and achieve goals, and so we are afraid to take risks. We feel responsible for things that go wrong, and when something goes right, we do not give ourselves credit. Instead, we feel undeserving and believe it is not going to last.

FEELINGS AND BEHAVIOR

1. NON-ASSERTIVENESS
2. FEAR OF FAILURE
3. INADEQUACY
4. FEAR OF REJECTION
5. ISOLATION
6. NEGATIVE SELF-IMAGE
7. PERFECTIONISM

RECOVERY FROM LOW SELF-ESTEEM

DESCRIPTION

As we build confidence in our abilities, our self-esteem increases. We are able to interact with others and to accept ourselves for who we really are. We see our good qualities, as well as our bad, and we learn to love ourselves. We become willing to take risks, and we realize we can achieve many things that we had never dreamed possible. Sharing feelings with others becomes more comfortable, and we feel safe allowing people to know us. Relationships become healthier because we no longer look to others for validation.

FEELINGS AND BEHAVIOR

1. SELF-CONFIDENCE
2. ASSERTIVENESS
3. INTERACT WITH OTHERS
4. SELF-LOVE
5. EXPRESS FEELINGS
6. TAKE RISKS

OVERDEVELOPED SENSE OF RESPONSIBILITY

DESCRIPTION

As children in a dysfunctional home, we felt responsible for what happened. We tried to be "model children" in order to solve our parents' problems. We developed the belief that we are responsible for the emotions and actions of others; even the outcome of events. We are hypersensitive to the needs of others, and we make an effort to take responsibility for others. It is important to us to be as perfect as possible. We volunteer to do things so that people will appreciate us. Our sense of responsibility causes us to overcommit, and we have a tendency to assume more than we are capable of handling.

FEELINGS AND BEHAVIOR

1. TAKE LIFE TOO SERIOUSLY
2. RIGIDITY
3. FALSE PRIDE
4. IRRESPONSIBLE
5. HIGH ACHIEVER
6. SUPER-RESPONSIBLE
7. PERFECTIONISM

RECOVERY FROM OVERDEVELOPED SENSE OF RESPONSIBILITY

DESCRIPTION

Accepting the fact that we are not responsible for others allows us time to take care of ourselves. We understand that we do not have an influence on the lives of others, and thus we realize that people are responsible for their own actions. As we take responsibility for our own actions, we become aware that we must take care of our own needs and rely on our Higher Power for guidance. We find time to support and nurture ourselves, as well as others.

FEELINGS AND BEHAVIOR

1. TAKE CARE OF SELF
2. ENJOY LEISURE TIME
3. ACCEPT OUR SHORTCOMINGS

SEXUALITY

DESCRIPTION

We find ourselves confused and uncertain about our sexual feelings toward others, particularly those we are close to or those with whom we desire to be emotionally intimate. We have been trained to think of our sexual feelings as unnatural, or abnormal. Because we do not share our feelings with others, we have no opportunity to develop a healthy attitude about our own sexuality. As small children, we may have explored our physical sexuality with peers and been punished for our transgressions. The message was "sex is dirty, not talked about, and is to be avoided."

Some of us saw our parents as nonsexual beings and believed we were the result of a "virgin birth." We may have been molested by a parent or close relative who was out of control because of excessive drinking or substance abuse. We are uncomfortable in our sexual role and may be sexually unsatisfied. We are inhibited from discussing sex with our partner for fear that our partner will not understand and will abandon us. If we have children, we may avoid discussions about sexuality and deny their need for sexual identity.

FEELINGS AND BEHAVIOR

1. LUST
2. INCEST
3. SEXUAL OBSESSION
4. SEDUCTIVE
5. SEXUAL IDENTITY CONFUSION
6. LOSS OF MORALITY
7. FRIGIDITY
8. IMPOTENCE

RECOVERY FROM SEXUALITY

DESCRIPTION

By relying upon the consistent love of our Higher Power, our self-worth increases. As we increase our self-love and our ability to take care of ourselves, we seek out healthy people who love and take care of themselves. We are no longer afraid of commitment and are better prepared to enter into a healthy relationship—emotionally, intellectually, and sexually. We feel more secure in sharing our feelings, strengths, and weaknesses. Our self-confidence grows and allows us to be vulnerable. We give up the need for perfection in ourselves and in others and, in so doing, open ourselves to discussion and change. We are honest about our own sexuality in discussions with our children, and we accept their need for information and sexual identity development.

FEELINGS AND BEHAVIOR

1. HONEST EXPRESSION OF FEELINGS
2. CONSIDERATION OF OUR OWN NEEDS
3. SHARE INTIMATE FEELINGS
4. SELF-CONFIDENCE
5. ACCCEPTANCE OF SEXUAL SELF

CHARACTER TRAIT EXERCISE

Use the following characteristics, to identify your actions when displaying character defects. Review what you wrote in your inventory and note the ways in which the following characteristics appear.

1. **PRIDE:** Inordinate self-esteem. Disdainful behavior or treatment.

2. **GREED** (Selfishness): Excessive or reprehensible acquisitiveness. Not having enough. Energy focused on having our way. To get our way, we injure others in the process.

3. **LUST** (Lechery): An intense desire, need, or sexual urge. Often motivated by fear of rejection.

4. **DISHONESTY** (Deceit): Disposition to defraud or deceive. Justifying our behaviors to others by explaining ourselves dishonestly.

5. **GLUTTONY** (Covetousness): One given habitually to greedy or voracious eating or drinking. Fear of rejection or worthlessness.

6. **ENVY** (Jealousy): Painful or resentful awareness of an advantage enjoyed by another, joined with a desire to possess the same advantage. Belief may be that one person is the source of one's love.

7. **LAZINESS:** Disinclined to activity or exertion; not energetic or vigorous. Fear of responsibility.

In recovery we replace fear with faith and deepen our trust in our Higher Power. We view ourselves as a combination of desirable and less desirable traits. We accept ourselves and all that we find within us.

1. **HUMILITY** (Modesty): Admit powerlessness and unmanageability as we accept our strengths and weaknesses.

2. **GENEROSITY** (Sharing): Feeling good about ourselves empowers us to care about the welfare and happiness of others.

3. **CONFIDENCE AND ACCEPTANCE OF SEXUAL SELF:** Feeling comfortable being sensuous, without having it lead to sexual intercourse. Clearly expressing preferences for sexual activity with partner.

4. **HONESTY:** Telling the truth, adhering to the facts, and responding to questions about our behavior with a feeling of security and self confidence.

5. **TEMPERANCE:** Moderation in activities, thoughts, or feelings. Stop using food or drink to avoid feelings or to conceal low self-esteem.

6. **AMICABLE, TRUSTFUL:** Encouragement and enthusiasm expressed toward others.

7. **ENERGETIC:** Self-starter; handle tasks without having to be told. Lively, prompt. Pay attention to work; find easier or simpler ways to do tasks.

STEP FIVE

ADMITTED TO GOD, TO OURSELVES, AND TO ANOTHER HUMAN BEING THE EXACT NATURE OF OUR WRONGS

Some of the truths of our lives were revealed in Step Four. The task of taking inventory was not easy. It demanded honesty, thoroughness, and balance. It took great courage to face the facts we discovered about ourselves by venturing into uncharted areas. If completed honestly, Step Four brought to light unresolved feelings, unhealed memories, and personal defects that have produced resentment, depression, and loss of self-worth. This process helped us confront the denial and self-deception that have been patterns in our lives.

Thoroughness in the Fourth Step helped us to see things as they really are. If we worked hard to uncover all the facts and did so thoroughly, Step Five will be more effective and rewarding. Balance in the Fourth Step inventory meant focusing on our strengths and weaknesses. Step Four helped to boost our self-esteem because we accepted all aspects of ourselves. For those who have been honest, thorough, and balanced, the writing of Step Four has been a gratifying experience. It has exposed us to many new discoveries and has provided us with a great sense of relief.

It is important to recognize that the relationship we have with our Higher Power is the source and foundation of our courage to enter into the task ahead of us. Reliance on our

Higher Power will help us become more willing to take risks. This willingness makes it possible for us to proceed with Step Five.

A good Fifth Step is possible after the successful completion of Step Four. We have accepted the reality of our character defects and the influence they have had on our lives. Having made a searching and fearless moral inventory, we are in a good position to complete the requirements of Step Five.

We will be telling our life story to three individuals—God, ourselves, and another human being. It is important to tell all that needs to be told so that we cleanse our being and are ready to move toward a deepened sense of spirituality. We may experience removal of guilt and feel like a weight has been lifted. Some of us will feel cleansed and renewed.

Step Five is a pathway out of isolation and loneliness. It is a step toward wholeness, happiness, and a real sense of gratitude. It questions our humility. Are we truly humble in the sense that we see ourselves as one of many human beings, all as children of God? If we are humble, we will feel secure and self-accepting when admitting to God the exact nature of our wrongs. Humility will also allow us to shift the weight of the Fifth Step onto our Higher Power and experience success in working the Fifth Step.

Step Five has three distinct parts. Admitting the exact nature of our wrongs to ourselves is the least threatening part and can be done with minimal risk. It does not provide an arena for testing our honesty or for seeing our own self-deception. Talking to ourselves holds back our ability to see ourselves in a realistic perspective. Fooling ourselves has been a pattern of our lives. Being alone with our own thoughts and feelings keeps us isolated and is limiting in nature. This isolation not only keeps others out, it keeps us in. The admission of our wrongs to ourselves prepares us for our conversation with God.

Step Five is an advancement toward ultimate surrender to a Higher Power, "Letting Go and Letting God." We must give up our desire to control the outcome. We must be willing to surrender the past and turn it over to a compassionate God who is understanding and forgiving. Admitting our wrongs to God is not for His benefit. It is an opportunity for us to realize that our Higher Power already knows us and is patiently waiting for us to confess how we still try to run the show. Trusting that our Higher Power is loving and forgiving, we become willing to admit our character defects to Him. In doing this, we experience a deepening sense of self-acceptance.

Nothing draws us to each other like honesty and humility. These qualities represent true humanity, which is what really attracts us to others. If we have been humble and honest with God and ourselves, completing the final stage of Step Five will be relatively easy. We need only find the right person with whom to share our wrongs.

The difficult part of Step Five is facing the need to admit our wrongs to another human being. This can be a frightening experience—to allow another person to see many parts of us that have been hidden behind our wall of self-deception. Some of our concerns may be that we will be laughed at or rejected for the horrors we reveal. This is a true test of our ability and willingness to be completely honest and to accept the consequences.

Decide on a dependable person, one familiar with the Program. Trusting the person we choose is essential to our success so that we can feel safe and unthreatened when exposing ourselves and our behavior. Sharing will flow easily if we understand one another and accept the limitations we all share as human beings. It is also important to recognize the unlimited forgiveness of our Higher Power.

When bringing our hidden thoughts to others, we need to do more than just be heard. We must be ready to listen to the other person's response. The interchange can be helpful and productive if we are willing to listen with an open mind to someone else's viewpoint. This broadens our awareness of ourselves and gives us an opportunity to change and grow. Feedback is vital to us as a means of completing the process of revelation. Questions asked in a caring and understanding manner can reveal feelings and situations that we were not aware of prior to sharing our life story.

When preparing for the Fifth Step, either as the participant or as the listener, the following suggestions are helpful:

As you prepare for Step Five, either as a participant or as a listener, the following suggestions are helpful.

1. Ask God's guidance in what you are undertaking. Ask Him to place you in an understanding and honest frame of mind that will make you open to what you are about to experience.
2. Allow sufficient time to complete each thought, but stay focused on the subject. Discourage unnecessary explanations.
3. Minimize distractions. Telephone calls, children, visitors, and extraneous noises can interfere with the flow of conversation.
4. Listen carefully. Ask questions if necessary so that the information is understood by both parties.
5. Remember that Step Five asks only that we admit the exact nature of our wrongs. It is not necessary to discuss how changes are going to be made.
6. Be supportive and acknowledge the person for the effort exerted in completing the Step.
7. When completed, each may share feelings about the experience and toward the other person.
8. Observe confidentiality. What you have shared with each other is not to be shared with anyone else. Nothing defeats honesty and damages relationships like a betrayed confidence.

Upon completion of Step Five, we may have expectations about where we should be in our process of recovery. How we feel is beside the point. We may not feel any differently than we did before. The real test of our Fifth Step admission is how willing we are to change our ways.

We realize that we are not always in control of things. Longstanding habits may have weakened our will to such an extent that it is extremely difficult to break our behavior patterns. We need to be realistic and understand that admitting the exact nature of our wrongs is not insurance against future lapses. We can expect to have lapses and still know that our relationship with our Higher Power will help us to face and overcome them.

It is not our intentions that matter. If we sincerely desire to change our ways, all God asks is that we pick ourselves up one more time than we fall. The end result of making our admission is not "results" so much as an experience of the reality of God's love.

STEP SIX

**WERE ENTIRELY
READY TO HAVE GOD
REMOVE ALL THESE
DEFECTS OF
CHARACTER**

Our success in working Steps One through Five is an indication of our readiness to complete Step Six. Steps One and Two prepared us for Step Three, at which time we made a decision to turn our will and our lives over to the care of God as we understood Him. Steps Four and Five helped us to uncover our defects of character. We faced them courageously and shared them with God, ourselves, and another human being. We have acknowledged our shortcomings without guilt because we have learned that blaming and punishing ourselves stunts our growth. The guilt feelings are natural, but to cling to them will keep us at a standstill. Step Six is another opportunity to turn our will over. The trust we have developed in, and our current feelings toward, our Higher Power is an encouraging prospect for having our character defects removed.

The character traits we have identified as defects are deeply ingrained patterns of behavior. They are tools we have acquired and used for survival in our daily lives. As we become aware of these defects and accept them, we can deal with them from a position of strength with the help of our Higher Power. Sharing our awareness of our defects honestly with

41

our Higher Power and trusting that He will help us remove them is the foundation of our strength and hope.

In our culture, self-will is a highly valued trait. We are taught from an early age that we should try to improve ourselves. Our parents, teachers, and employers have told us that it is our duty to them and to God that we work on our own defects. As a result, we use our self-will to accumulate and demonstrate success. It is a rare person who attributes his or her success to the existence of a Higher Power, and surrenders to Him.

We are often comfortable with some of our defects. They have been familiar tools to us. The thought of having them removed can be threatening to our security. As difficult as it may seem, we must be willing to let go of these defects in order to become entirely ready to have God remove them. Being entirely ready requires a dedication like that illustrated in preparing for a race, learning to speak in front of an audience, or developing skills as an artist. Certain tasks must be performed in order to succeed.

Preparing to be entirely ready to have God remove our defects of character is accomplished through the training we have undergone in the first Five Steps. We have inadvertently begun to experience confidence in the ongoing process of working and living the Steps one day at a time. Being entirely ready implies trust, faith, and belief that the one we are going to ask will fulfill our request.

One of the most important ingredients in preparing for Step Six is humility. We must relinquish our egos, truly seek God's will for us, and let go of our own. Our trust in God tells us that He will remove only the defects that are necessary. The way to learn what God has in mind for us is to be ready for God to remove our desire for things that are not good for us.

The task of removing all of our character defects is more than we can handle; we are not able to do it alone. Step Six does not say we have to do the removing. All we have to do is allow it to happen, let go. It is not an action step that we actually take. It is a state of being that takes us. One day we realize that we no longer have any qualms about letting God remove any and all of our character defects as He sees fit.

This we do by faithfully working the Program, day by day, whether we feel like we're making progress or not.

For some of the more deeply rooted defects, we may find it necessary to become a detached observer. By becoming an observer of our behavior and of the behavior of others, we notice how we act or react in various situations. When we see ourselves thinking negatively or doing something that is not constructive, we can make a note of it and ask for help from our Higher Power. By doing this, the task will become much easier.

Some people reach a state of preparedness quickly and are ready to have God remove all of their character defects. For most of us, the process is slow and gradual. When we cling to old habits and unproductive ways of thinking, we block the process of change and the flow of inspiration. One way to use God's help is to allow solutions to come to us by turning to our Higher Power. This can be done by saying the Serenity Prayer as often as necessary.

It may be beneficial to analyze our communication with God. The following statements are examples of the distinction between asking and admitting. "Dear God, I want to be more patient" is making a demand and telling God what we want. "Dear God, I am impatient" is presenting the truth about ourselves. This allows God to make the decision for us based on our admission.

As we live the principles of the Program in our daily lives, we gradually and unconsciously become ready to have our defects of character removed. What sometimes happens is that we are not aware of being ready to have our defects removed or of asking God to remove them. The first awareness we have is that we are different somehow. We have changed. Often the change is noticed by others before we become aware of it ourselves. The approval-seeking person begins to function more adequately; the control addict becomes warmer and more relaxed; the super-responsible individual is no longer victimizing himself by doing for others what they can do for themselves. People who work the Program as an integral part of their lives become calmer, more serene, and wear genuine smiles. Much of the work we do in the Program is done without conscious action on our part.

There is a radiant, confident personality in each of us, hidden under a shroud of confusion, uncertainty, and defects. If someone were to ask if we wanted to be freed from our character defects, there could only be one answer—that we are entirely ready to have God remove them.

STEP SEVEN

HUMBLY ASKED HIM TO REMOVE OUR SHORTCOMINGS

Attainment of greater humility is the foundation principle of the ACA Twelve Step Program. It is through humility that we reach the goals as outlined in the Steps. The basic ingredient in humility as it applies to the program is a desire to seek and do God's will.

In working and living Steps One and Two, a degree of humility was necessary when we admitted our powerlessness and came to believe that a Power greater than ourselves could restore us to sanity. In Step Three, humility allowed us to turn our will and our lives over to the care of God as we understood Him. Without humility, Steps Four and Five would be extremely difficult. In Step Six, our being ready to have our defects removed was in direct proportion to the degree of our humility.

The entire emphasis in Step Seven is humility. This is the point at which we change our attitude and move from being self-centered to self-less. This produces harmony with God and other people. As we grow in the Program, we see humility as being absolutely necessary for survival. Humility is simply the growing awareness that "Of myself I am nothing, the Father doeth the work." Only by a deepening awareness of this can we humbly ask God to remove our shortcomings.

We desire humility because we realize that it is the only way to achieve the peace, serenity, and happiness we seek. If we desire to be a maturing, growing, useful, joyous person, we will have to develop an inner calm, even in a turbulent, insane world. To achieve this inner calm, we must develop the ability to accept things as they are when we cannot change them and to ask God for the courage to change the things we can.

Step Seven implies removal of all our shortcomings. It is important that we deal with them individually, preferably with the easiest ones first to build confidence in our progress. Our commitment to doing the footwork one day at a time supports the idea that progress will come at a comfortable pace with God's help. If we ask God to remove a character defect and it is not removed, we do not need to be discouraged or angry. We need to be patient and realize that we have more work to do. We may not be entirely ready to have it removed, or we may not have humbly asked God.

In preparing to have our defects removed, we must demonstrate our complete willingness on an ongoing basis. We must cooperate. We cannot expect our shortcomings to be removed if we continue to behave the way we did before and simply wait for God to do all the work. Even though we have asked, it is important to be aware of any tendencies to repeat old behavior. Anytime we become aware of the "old defects" at work, being gentle with ourselves at that moment is very important. God loves us however we are, and it is an opportunity for us to love ourselves. This is simply an indication that some part of us still wants to hang on, that we are learning to accept God's will, but that we are not yet humble enough to willingly let go.

Being open to the wisdom and guidance of our Higher Power is vital at this time. When meditating on the recurrence of behaviors that we consider "immature," it is wise to remind ourselves that our inner-child is "unmatured." If we are willing to grow spiritually and emotionally, we will see progress. Any improvement is cause for gratitude and joy. We need to remember that this process of spiritual development is lifelong, yet we practice it one day at a time or one minute at a time if necessary.

No matter how hard we try, we can never hope to eliminate all our character defects, in spite of all the praying we do for guidance. Achieving sainthood is not part of this program. We simply do the best we can. We are not expected to fit any image at all. We are only required to humbly ask that our shortcomings be removed.

Humbly asking God to remove our shortcomings is a true means of surrender and may be difficult for some of us. As M. Scott Peck pointed out in his book, *The Road Less Traveled*, depression often accompanies the process of releasing. "There are many factors that can interfere with the giving-up process and, therefore, prolong a normal, healthy depression into a chronic pathologic depression. Of all the possible factors, one of the most common and potent is a pattern of experiences in childhood wherein parents or fate, unresponsive to the needs of the child, took away 'things' from the child before he or she was psychologically ready to give them up or strong enough to truly accept their loss. Such a pattern of experience in childhood sensitizes the child to the experience of loss and creates a tendency far stronger than that found in more fortunate individuals to cling to 'things' and seek to avoid the pain of loss or giving up. For this reason, although all pathologic depressions involve some blockage in the giving-up process, I believe there is a type of chronic neurotic depression that has as its central root a traumatic injury to the individual's basic capacity to give up anything . . ."[2] Much of the work done in this book is to heal the pain of the inner-child.

Humbly asking a child to set the table for dinner, then impatiently doing it yourself can be likened to humbly asking God to remove your shortcomings, then insisting on removing them yourself. In neither case are you humbly asking for anything to be done. No one can truly take credit for removing any of their character defects. If we expect any credit, we are doomed to failure. Sudden changes can and do happen, but we cannot expect them or direct them. God causes them when we are ready for them. When we humbly ask God to do the removing, it becomes His responsibility and we cannot accept credit or blame for what follows.

The items that remain in our inventory after this process is completed must belong there. It is an opportunity for us to take these remaining "defects" and allow God to turn them into positive traits. With God's help, this can be a rewarding and exciting experience. Natural leaders may be left with a quest for power but with no desire to misuse it. Natural lovers will be left with exquisite sensuality but with enough consideration not to hurt anyone with it. Those who are meant to be materially wealthy will be, but without greed and possessiveness.

In order to work the Program successfully, we must practice The Steps on a daily basis until it becomes a routine. In this way, we will eventually be capable of breaking the bonds of our old and unhealthy habits and behaviors. We will begin to trust the thoughts and feelings that show up as a result of our conscious contact with God. We will come to know that the guidance we receive from our Higher Power is always available; all we need to do is listen and act without fear.

SEVENTH STEP PRAYER

"My Creator, I am now willing that you should have all of me, good and bad. I pray that you now remove from me every single defect of character which stands in your way of my usefulness to you and my fellow. Grant me the strength, as I go out from here, to do your bidding. Amen."[3]

Big Book (A.A.)

SERENITY PRAYER

"God, grant me the serenity
To accept the things I cannot change,
The courage to change the things I can,
And the wisdom to know the difference."

2. M. Scott Peck, M.D., *The Road Less Traveled*, (New York: Simon and Schuster, Inc.), p. 70.
3. Alcoholics Anonymous, Alcoholics Anonymous World Services, Inc. (New York), p.76.

STEP EIGHT

MADE A LIST OF ALL PERSONS WE HAD HARMED, AND BECAME WILLING TO MAKE AMENDS TO THEM ALL

Step Eight is the beginning of the end of our isolation from our fellows and from God. Relationships are what Step Eight and Nine are all about—our relationships with other people, with ourselves, and with our Higher Power. In this step, we must show a desire and willingness to write down each of our past misdeeds, the dates, and the names of those people involved. We cannot remake the present until we undo the past. This is done gradually by gently loving ourselves as we mature and by allowing our inner child to grow up.

The first Seven Steps are "personal" in that they are concerned with an examination of our behavior patterns and are intended to make us aware of our personal experiences. By the time we reach this point in recovery, we are beginning to see how important it is for us to let go of the past with its painful and sometimes pleasurable memories. Through these changes in our awareness, we learn to live each day in harmony with ourselves and others. Releasing the past opens the path to a new life for us, a life based on living one day at a time.

In order to find enjoyment in recovery, it is important that we develop the ability to overcome guilt, shame, resentment, low self-worth, and fear of other people. To accomplish this may seem like an awesome task since we have probably tried to do it before. This time, however, we have the opportunity to restore our personal integrity and self-authority by working the Steps. We can trust in the process because it has worked miracles for millions of people.

The first part of Step Eight specifically states that we make a list of those we have harmed. When making the list, many of us may hit a solid obstacle. It can be a severe shock to realize that we must make a face-to-face admission of our past wrongs to those we have harmed. It was embarrassing enough to admit them to ourselves, to God, and to another human being in Step Five. In Step Nine, we actually have to visit or write the people concerned.

Those who have successfully worked the first Five Steps are usually aware of those they have harmed by the time they reach Step Eight. You may discover that the person you have harmed most is yourself. Sometimes we realize that we have become our own worst enemy, and our resentment against ourselves manifests itself in the form of excessive self-blame, guilt, and sometimes shame. Guilt is an appropriate response to regrets over actions in conflict with our personal values. Shame is excessive guilt and may cause us to view ourselves as bad or worthless, which is unhealthy.

When starting Step Eight, make a list of the people you feel uncomfortable with. Just make a list. Don't worry about the details. Making the list enables us to go where our mind takes us. Our list may start with family members, business associates, friends, creditors, and neighbors. Its length is not important, yet it may reveal a somewhat unrealistic view of the power of our personal influence. Step Eight is another exercise in preparation for the ongoing process of healing that this Program offers. The powerful elixir of honesty is what makes the healing take place.

In order to complete this Step, we must be willing to face the facts and make amends. We must be ready to willingly accept the consequences and take whatever measures are necessary to make restitution. This may be difficult for some of us because it means fully and completely acknowledging our part of every dispute in which harm has come to someone as a result of our action or inaction. We need to do this, regardless of cause, no matter how justified we may have felt.

Only by expressing genuine regret for our own part in the dispute can we complete our housecleaning. This housecleaning is necessary for us to develop spiritually and to achieve the peace and serenity we desire.

Forgiveness is the next key factor in completing Step Eight. We must be willing to forgive ourselves as well as those who we feel have caused us harm. This takes a great deal of humility on our part. We have already become aware that resentments and grudges are luxuries we cannot afford. They not only destroy our serenity and sanity, but they are more harmful to us than to the person we resent. A resentment or grudge is like an open sore eating away at our insides, making us grouchy, bitter, ill-tempered, and unable to concentrate on growth because our energy is spent on our grudge or resentment.

The most effective means of overcoming resentment is forgiveness of ourselves and of others. Forgiveness of others begins when we become aware of our own contributions to the difficulties in our relationships. Looking at ourselves helps us become willing to release our anger and our condemnation of others. Through acceptance, forgiveness, and turning it over to our Higher Power, we will be able to rid ourselves of these grudges and resentments. When we understand the damage we have done, we need to make amends and reduce our likelihood of repeating this pattern of behavior. If we do not forgive ourselves, we cannot forgive others. If we do not forgive others, we cannot make amends with dignity, self-respect, and humility. Amends without forgiveness can lead us into a new argument or dispute. Our willingness to make amends must stem from a true desire for forgiveness.

When looking back at those we have harmed, we see how our character defects have played a major part in sabotaging ourselves and others. The following are examples of this behavior:

1. When we became angry, we often harmed ourselves more than we did others.
2. When confronted with an issue about which we felt guilt and were in denial, we lashed out at the other person rather than looking at ourselves.

3. Frustrated by our lack of control, we behaved badly and intimidated those around us.
4. Our fear of abandonment sometimes destroyed relationships, because we did not allow the other person to be himself; rather, we smothered him in an effort to maintain the relationship.

Humility can help us see each human being as having an equal right to be here and to live as happily as we do. This does not mean we have to agree with everyone about everything, but it does mean we can stop hating people for what they have done and stop resenting them because their views are different from ours. Our own sanity will be preserved, and our serenity greatly enhanced, if we can forgive and even love our enemies rather than hate them or wish them harm.

As we proceed through the Steps, we do indeed learn to forgive, like, and love the enemy within us. As we learn to understand our inner enemy and accept him, our spiritual growth will advance at a rapid pace. As we forgive our outer enemies, they become less enemies and, in some cases, become close friends.

If we are willing to make amends and to face our past, we become more tolerant and forgiving, less rigid and judgmental. We will begin to realize that our Higher Power is doing for us what we could not do for ourselves. At this point, we are beginning to experience real changes in our viewpoints, attitudes, and beliefs, and we are becoming ready and willing to participate in the process of reconciliation. Now we are ready to move on the Step Nine and actually make the amends we have found necessary.

AMENDS LIST

Following are three main categories in which we may have caused harm and for which we must be willing to make amends.

MATERIAL WRONGS: Your actions affecting an individual in a tangible way, such as one of the following:

1. Money—borrowing or spending extravagance; stinginess; spending in an attempt to buy friendship or love; withholding money in order to gratify yourself.
2. Contracts—entering into an agreement that is legally enforceable, then not abiding by the terms, or simply cheating (e.g. a business transaction that is to provide products or services—agreeing to repay loans or make payments on time).
3. Person or Property—any injury or damage as a result of your action.
4. Personal Abuse—physical or sexual.

MORAL WRONGS: Dealing with what is right and wrong in behavior as well as in moral duty or obligation. Also including the questions of rightness, fairness, or equity. The principal issue is involving others in your wrongdoing:

1. Setting a bad example for children, friends, or anyone who looked to you for guidance.
2. Excessive preoccupation with selfish pursuits and using justification as your way to deny your actions. This caused you to be totally unaware of the needs of others. (e.g. preoccupation resulted in lost caring for, or attention to, children or relationship partner. Another example would be obsession with an addictive partner, possibly causing job ineffectiveness.)
3. Being forgetful of special occasions (e.g. birthdays and holidays pass unnoticed).
4. Moral harms (e.g. sexual infidelity, broken promises, verbal abuse, lack of trust, unkind criticism, lying).

SPIRITUAL WRONGS: Principally, "acts of omission" that are the neglect of obligations to God, to yourself, family, and to community.

1. Making no effort to fulfill your obligations and showing a lack of gratitude toward others who have stepped in for you (e.g. family and children, work tasks).
2. Avoiding self-development (Example: health, education, recreation, creativity).
3. Being inattentive to others in your life by showing a lack of encouragement to them.

STEP NINE

**MADE DIRECT
AMENDS TO SUCH
PEOPLE WHEREVER
POSSIBLE, EXCEPT
WHEN TO DO SO
WOULD INJURE THEM
OR OTHERS**

Step Nine is another action step and again requires that we demonstrate a willingness to confront issues of our past, which may have been dormant for a long time. This Step clearly requires courage and a renewed understanding of our intention to free ourselves from the guilt we may feel for any hurt done to others. The benefits to us are certainly worth taking the risk of making amends.

Engaging in this process of forgiveness is like having spiritual surgery performed on us. The distant memories, which may still be painful and linger in our minds, can encumber us. They diminish our vitality and joy for living. Making amends somehow seems to make many of these memories simply disappear. Being attached to someone in our memory as a result of an uncomfortable experience and, then, making amends with that person, can be likened to the release of a butterfly trapped in the hands of a curious child. Letting go allows both to explore and move about in their own independent and natural state. It also allows for a new relationship to emerge.

Good judgment, a careful sense of timing, courage, and prudence are qualities that we will need when taking Step Nine. It is wise to reflect upon the intended amends for a while.

Our objective is not to buy our peace of mind at the expense of others. Forethought will prepare us for the appropriate time and deter us from causing any further harm. The process may include seeking guidance from a trusted friend as well as humbly asking our Higher Power for guidance, support, and the willingness to do whatever is necessary.

Step Nine requires that direct amends be made wherever possible. We must be careful not to procrastinate by telling ourselves the time is not right. We may be tempted to skip the more humiliating and dreaded meetings or to find excuses to dodge the issues entirely. We must be sure that we are not delaying because of fear. Fear is lack of courage, and courage is an important part of this Step. The readiness to accept the full consequences of our past and, at the same time, take responsibility for the well-being of others is the very spirit of Step Nine.

Amends will be possible with almost everyone, even those who may not be aware of what we have done to them. In every word or action that violates the Golden Rule, "Do unto others as we would have them do unto us," there are amends to make. If someone is unable to accept a restitution, their part of the problem will have to remain unresolved, and our using the Serenity Prayer will be helpful for our own peace of mind.

When looking at making amends, we see that the Step has two distinct parts:

"MADE DIRECT AMENDS TO SUCH PEOPLE WHEREVER POSSIBLE,"

People who need to be dealt with as soon as possible and are readily accessible.

These people include family members, employees or employers, or creditors to whom we owe financial amends. They may include friends as well as enemies. It is harder to go to an enemy than to a friend, but we will find it much more beneficial to us. When we are ready to face the consequences of our past, we will be able to go to them, admit the damage we have done, and make our apologies. The generous response of most people to such sincerity will often astonish us. Even our severest and most justified critics will frequently meet us more than halfway on the first attempt.

Situations whose very nature will never allow us to make direct personal contact.

This may involve people who are no longer a part of our lives or who have died. In these cases, indirect amends can satisfy our need to make things right. We can make indirect amends through prayer or by writing a letter, as if we are actually communicating with the person. Indirect amends can also be made by doing a kindness for someone else's child or parent when we no longer have any responsibility for caring for the person. We can make amends to our adult children by respecting them as adults, by maintaining our own recovery, and by being healthy and reasonably happy adults ourselves.

"EXCEPT WHEN TO DO SO WOULD INJURE THEM OR OTHERS."

People to whom we can only make partial restitution because complete disclosure could cause harm to them or others.

These people may include our spouses, ex-partners, former business associates, or friends. We must analyze the harm that could come to them if complete amends were made. This is especially true in cases where infidelity is present in a marriage. Amends in this area can cause irreparable damage to all parties concerned. Even in cases where the matter can be discussed, we should avoid harming third parties. It does not lighten our burden when we make the crosses of others harder to bear. Amends for unfaithfulness can be made indirectly by a change in behavior, or by concentrating more sincere affection and attention on the one who has been deceived.

In cases involving serious consequences, such as potential loss of employment, imprisonment, or other harm to one's family, each one of us has to make the decision carefully. We should not be deterred from making amends by fear for ourselves but only by the real possibility of injury to others. If we choose to delay making amends out of fear, we will be the ones to suffer in the end. We will delay our growth, experience regression, become more emotionally ill, and possibly return to our prior insane behavior.

Situations where action should be deferred.

In these areas, it can be helpful to seek other counsel when we assess our judgment of the situation. It is seldom wise to approach an individual who still smarts from the injustices we have done. In situations where our own hurts are still deeply imbedded, patience might prove to be wise. We can know that amends must be made eventually, but our timing is important so that we can gain and grow from the experience.

When you actually start the process of making amends, be careful not to confuse apologies with amends. Apologies are sometimes called for, but apologies are not amends. We may discover in apologizing that we explain excessively, and this is not as effective as simply changing. Amends are made by acting differently. We can apologize a hundred times for being late for work, but this will not "mend" the tardiness. Appearing at work on time is a change in behavior, and thus becomes an amend.

Occasional emotional or spiritual relapses, or "slips," are to be expected and need to be dealt with in a timely manner. When these relapses occur, we must accept them as signals that we are forgetting something. Perhaps we have taken part of our will back from our Higher Power and need to go back to Step Three; or possibly we have eliminated something from our inventory and must go back to Step Four; or we may have a character defect that we are not willing to let go of and must return to Step Six.

In reality, the entire Twelve Step Program is one of constant repetition and gradual improvement. Most of us need to go over the Steps regularly throughout our lifetime. After the first time, the Steps do not need to be repeated in order. As we grow spiritually, we will be able to rely on them as one of the major factors in our journey toward recovery and a spiritual awakening.

In repairing the damage we have done to others, we will also be overhauling our own lives. If we do it thoroughly, we can find ourselves returned to an amazingly peaceful state without hatred, guilt, or resentment. We will feel a glow of satisfaction in knowing we have honestly done everything we can to pay off every material, moral, and spiritual debt we owe to our fellow human beings.

The importance of Step Nine is obvious. It finally gives us the chance to eradicate past concerns and to start living in the present. We have taken the opportunity to balance good with evil, and it will make us feel good about ourselves. As difficult as it may have been to make amends and to replace our misery with happiness, the joy we try to give will not measure up to the pleasure this Step gives us.

We are now in a place to rebuild self-esteem, achieve unity with self and others, increase self-acceptance and self-respect, and be in harmony with God and with out own personal world.

GUIDELINES TO USE FOR MAKING AMENDS TO OTHERS

ATTITUDE

1. Be willing to love and forgive yourself and the person to whom the amends are made.
2. Know what you want to say and be careful not to blame the person in your communication.
3. Take responsibility for what you are going to say.
4. Be willing to accept the outcome.
5. Don't expect a particular response from the other person.
6. Be willing to turn it over to God.

PREPARATION

1. Devote time to prayer and meditation. If you are angry or upset, delay the amend and do more Step Four inventory work.
2. Keep it simple. Details and explanations aren't necessary.
3. Remember that the amend does not pertain to the other person's part in the situation.
4. Express your desire or ask permission to make amends. Example:

   > "I am involved in a program that suggests I be aware of the harm I have done to others and that I need to take responsibility for my actions. I'd like to make amends to you. Are you OK to receive it?"

SAMPLE AMENDS

1. I was (scared, overwhelmed, feeling abandoned, etc.) when _____ happened between us. I ask your forgiveness for ___*(harm done)*___ and for anything else I may have done in the past that caused you pain either by my thoughts, words, or actions. I didn't intend to cause you pain and I ask your forgiveness.
2. I want to make an amend to you about _____ . For all those words that were said out of (fear, thoughtlessness, etc.) and out of my confusion, I ask your forgiveness.

GUIDELINES TO USE FOR MAKING AMENDS TO YOURSELF

ATTITUDE
1. Be willing to love and forgive yourself.
2. Know what you want to say and take responsibility for your actions.
3. Don't have unreasonable expectations of yourself.
4. Be willing to turn it over to God.

PREPARATION
1. Devote time to prayer and meditation. Delay the amend if you are angry or upset, and do more Step Four inventory work.
2. Keep it simple. Explanations are not necessary.
3. Remember the amend is to yourself and don't be concerned with the other persons involved.

SAMPLE AMENDS
1. I was (scared, overwhelmed, feeling abandoned, etc.) when _____ happened. I forgive myself for the __(harm done)__ and anything else I may have done in the past by my thoughts, words, or actions that may have caused me harm.
2. I want to make an amend to myself about _____ . I forgive myself for all the words that I said out of (fear, thoughtlessness, etc.) and out of my own confusion.

STEP TEN

**CONTINUED TO TAKE
PERSONAL
INVENTORY AND,
WHEN WE WERE
WRONG, PROMPTLY
ADMITTED IT**

The initial work we have done with the Steps shows us the ineffective behavior we have been using for a considerable length of time. For many of us, the Steps may have served as an antidote to relieve some of the pain of our addictive behavior. Our commitment to continue working the Steps is an acknowledgment of our intention to improve the quality of our lives and our relationships.

Having completed Steps One through Nine, our initial housecleaning is complete, and we can begin the maintenance, sustenance, and growth phases of the Program—Steps Ten, Eleven, and Twelve. It has become apparent that spiritual growth is a lifelong process; our program must be maintained on a daily basis, one day at a time. When we accept the notion that the healing process is for the rest of our lives, the urgency to get through this work diminishes.

Some of us get the illusion that after we have completed the first Nine Steps, we are home free. We are comfortable with ourselves and no longer see a need to attend meetings regularly. We allow other activities to come into our lives, which interfere with our attending meetings, and we find excuses for missing meetings, such as being tired or having to drive too far. Some of us drop out completely. If we choose this path, we will eventually realize that our recovery is in jeopardy. We may become irritable, short-tempered, or negative in our attitudes.

At some point, we may begin to wonder if our new problems are related to the missed meetings. When we decide to return to the meetings, we will see the warmth and enthusiasm that is present. The emotional and spiritual uplift we will feel can help us get back on the path. Once we accept that we cannot afford to give up the Program, we will feel a gentle inner force compelling us to continue to develop further, to grow spiritually, one day at a time, beyond all imaginable boundaries.

Step Ten suggests that we continue to take personal inventory and, when wrong, promptly admit it. This is an important process in our recovery; we cannot afford to hang on to useless, harmful attitudes and practices. We need to be on the lookout for signs of trying to manage our lives alone, thereby slipping into past patterns such as resentment, fear, dishonesty, or selfishness. When we see our defects crop up, it's time to ask God to remove them at once, discuss them with someone, and make amends promptly if we have caused harm.

In order to successfully complete the remaining Steps of the Program, we need to acknowledge fully our need for continued spiritual development. Just as our stomachs tell us when it is time to eat, so do our souls tell us when it is time for spiritual nourishment. We recognize that we must take care of ourselves emotionally and spiritually. We begin to appreciate and love ourselves as being whole and complete. We are able to see long-range possibilities for our future successes. With the help of our Higher Power, we are able to "Let Go and Let God" so that our stress is minimized. Daily practice of Step Ten maintains our honesty and humility and allows us to continue our development.

The Program suggests three types of ongoing inventories.

SPOT-CHECK INVENTORY
This is a short review of our actions, thoughts, and motives done several times a day as the need arises. Taking frequent

inventories and promptly admitting our wrongs keeps us free from guilt and supports our spiritual growth.

During our daily activities, it is sometimes hard to recognize that seemingly nice actions are actually a signal that our old behavior is returning. An example of this is when we do a favor for someone. In the process, we think that no one else would take the time to do what we are doing. This triggers a feeling of superiority and tends to make us feel self-righteous. It can also be a sign that we are still seeking approval by "people-pleasing."

Another tendency is to see a wrong we are doing and blame someone else. We become angry and sometimes lose our tempers. We justify our anger rather than take responsibility for our behavior. In the end, we realize that our anger was not necessarily related to the other person's actions. It was a result of our own fears, anxieties, and feelings of insecurity.

DAILY INVENTORY

A daily review of the day's activities serves different and complementary purposes. It reminds us that this is a daily program, lived one day at a time. It keeps us focused on today and helps prevent us from worrying about the future or living in the past. We take this inventory much the same as in Step Four, except we are concerned only with today. The review is usually a "quickie" done on the run or just before we go to sleep.

As we take our daily inventory, questions arise, and we try to be as honest and humble as possible. Some of the questions we might ask ourselves are as follows:

1. Are we slipping back into control and manipulation, and are we trying to arrange the outcome of events? It is important that we recognize our behavior and ask God to correct it.

2. Are we comparing ourselves to others and feeling inferior, thus causing us to isolate ourselves? We need to reach out to our supportive friends and to acknowledge our current state, thereby renewing our self-acceptance.

3. Are we becoming obsessive/compulsive and not taking care of ourselves? Although we dislike "pressure," we

may still put ourselves under all types of stress. This is a signal to slow down and proceed with moderation.

4. Are we frightened by angry people and authority figures, and do we hesitate to stand up to them? We need to remind ourselves that our ultimate authority figure, our Higher Power, is always with us.

5. Are we becoming caretakers and feeling responsible for all persons and all things? We must remember that we are responsible only for ourselves.

6. Are we depressed? If so, we need to examine the core issue that is causing us to feel sorry for ourselves.

7. Are we withholding our true feelings and finding it difficult to express our wants and needs, or are we simply giving in to others? We must overcome this so that frozen feelings do not become a pattern of behavior.

LONG-TERM PERIODIC INVENTORY

This is done once or twice a year and gives us a chance to reflect on our progress from a better perspective. We can see the remarkable changes we have made, which give us a great deal of satisfaction. We must be careful not to inflate our egos, and we must remind ourselves that our progress is a reflection of our spiritual growth. Long-term inventories help us to recognize problem areas and make the necessary corrections. We sometimes find brand new defects as a result of our new experiences.

When a character defect reappears or a new one is identified, we can do an inventory, keeping in mind the following points:

1. Repeating patterns are old choices of our subconscious mind and are founded upon struggle, helplessness, guilt, revenge, and disapproval.

2. We feel safe when something is familiar, even though it is an addiction from the past.

3. We victimize ourselves by allowing the past to possess us. We can let go of the past with the help of our Higher Power.

4. Clinging to any character defects is a sure way to keep ourselves from obtaining what we want.

5. Releasing an old character trait is frightening. By surrendering to our Higher Power, we can trust that we will be given one that is appropriate.

6. Reach out. Your loving, supportive friends are an important ingredient to recovery and are available to us throughout our Program.

It is to be expected that our inventories will show us where we are slipping into old behavior patterns. The wrong we must admit is that we violated our contract with God, which we made in the Third Step. When we turned our wills and our lives over to God's care, we agreed that we would accept God's will for us. Now we must admit that we have repossessed our wills and our lives, and we must return to Step Three. It is important to realize that pride and fear are always working to keep us from the painful task of dealing with our own faults.

Good Step Ten work has many benefits and rewards, most important of which is that it strengthens and protects our recovery. It brings rewards in several areas, such as:

1. *Personal relationships.* Troubled relationships seem to disappear. By taking inventory and admitting our wrongs promptly, the misunderstandings usually dissolve.

2. *Freedom from fear of "being found out."* Our refusal to admit wrongs is rooted in feelings of inferiority and inadequacy. We always needed to look right to other people. It is a relief to learn that we do not need to put up a false front any longer. It is okay to be ourselves.

3. *Freedom from guilt.* Guilt is one of the prices we pay for not admitting our wrongs. When we realize how harmful this is, we become more willing to face our wrongs and quickly admit them. At this point, the guilt can be removed.

4. *Ability to help others.* A surprising benefit of admitting our wrongs is that we become able to help others make similar admissions. When we admit our wrongs and stop accusing others, the way is shown to a real understanding of another's problems and to what the person can do about it.

A final thought about Step Ten is to pay special attention to acting promptly. The sooner we admit our wrongs, the sooner the harm can be repaired to ourselves as well as to others. Delay in admitting our wrongs shows resistance to practicing Step Ten. This can be harmful because matters usually become worse. Eternal vigilance in taking a Tenth Step inventory is the price of freedom. It is our path toward freedom, and it releases us to complete the final two steps and to obtain the serenity and spirituality we are looking for.

STEP ELEVEN

SOUGHT THROUGH PRAYER AND MEDITATION TO IMPROVE OUR CONSCIOUS CONTACT WITH GOD AS WE UNDERSTOOD HIM, PRAYING ONLY FOR KNOWLEDGE OF HIS WILL FOR US AND FOR THE POWER TO CARRY THAT OUT

Step Eleven is our opportunity to develop a deepening relationship with our Higher Power. Having developed this relationship in Steps Two and Three, we have been able to rely on it during the subsequent Steps. The relationship we developed with our Higher Power was the source of courage and strength for doing the work suggested in the Steps.

At this point in working the Twelve Steps, we have no doubt noticed that to "make a decision to turn our will and our lives over to the care of God" is not a single event. It is a daily routine. Now we are being asked to "pray for knowledge of His will for us and for the power to carry that out." Turning our will over may have been more of a challenge than seeking the knowledge of God's will for us because of our persistent and repeated feelings of distrust. We were first confronted with the power of our ego (self-will) in Step One. A psychiatrist and pioneer in the field of addiction, H.M. Tiebout, M.D., wrote that the ego is made up of the persisting elements, in the adult psyche, of the original nature of the child. When infantile traits continue into adulthood, the person is referred to as being immature. The ego is the arch-enemy of our emotional sobriety.

If we are periodically puzzled by the daily challenges we face from "His Majesty the Baby," we must accept that we are adult children and are still growing up. The inner child of our past tolerates frustration poorly, tends to want to do things in a nurry, and is impatient with delay. The hallmark in our adult life is the tendency to be under pressure for accomplishment. Big plans, schemes, and hopes abound, Unfortunately, these are not always matched by an ability to produce. We are clearly not doing God's will when we are expressing this behavior. "Like the cat with nine lives, the ego has a marvelous capacity to scramble back to safety—a little ruffled, perhaps, but soon operating with all its former aplomb, convinced once more that now it, the ego, can master all events and push on ahead."[4]

Doing God's will may get so entangled with the reassertion of our old feelings and attitudes that our emotional sobriety becomes a shambles of discontent and restlessness. As we see this struggle in process, the need for our Higher Power becomes clearer.

Step Eleven is where we focus on the daily process that is necessary for our spiritual awakening. We may have had spiritual experiences prior to this, but a spiritual experience is not a spiritual awakening. In fact, many spiritual experiences may be required before a spiritual awakening is possible. It is only through experience that the existence of a Power greater than ourselves is finally proven to us. A spiritual awakening comes when we know there is a Higher Power that has been taking care of our wills and our lives when we know and we can depend on that Higher Power to run the show from now on.

Step Eleven suggests that we improve our conscious contact with God as we understand Him. In order to do this, we must have already established contact. We have made conscious contact with God at least three times in the earlier Steps. In Step Three, we made a decision to turn our wills and our lives over to God's care. In Step Five, we admitted our wrongs directly to Him. In Step Seven, we humbly asked Him to remove our shortcomings. Step Eleven seeks to improve that contact, thereby enabling us to bring our Higher Power into our lives on a daily basis. It is now that we can begin to enjoy the quality relationship that is possible with Him.

The Program implies that our Higher Power is a loving power who has only the best interests of each individual in mind. The basic premise includes the idea that this loving power wants to enrich our lives. It is exciting to realize that we can have an abundant life if we accept the protection and care of our Higher Power. The A.A. pioneers believed that this abundant life could be had for the asking. "We found that God does not make too hard terms with those who seek Him. To us, the Realm of Spirit is broad, roomy, all inclusive; never exclusive or forbidding to those who earnestly seek. It is open, we believe, to all men."[5]

The means recommended to improve our conscious contact are prayer and meditation. These are the channels by which we reach Him and He reaches us. To pray is to petition God for what we would like Him to give us, and to ask for His guidance in our affairs. Prayer tells God what we want. Meditation is listening to God's will for us. Meditation techniques are designed to quiet our minds and rid us of our daily thoughts and concerns. In doing this, we allow God to enter into our minds so that we can hear His messages for us.

Assuming we are willing, how do we pray, and what do we pray for? Many of us were taught to pray before we understood what it meant. In the beginning, we may have used the prayer "Now I lay me down to sleep, etc." We asked God to bless Mommy and Daddy and significant others. As we grew up, our dysfunctional family experiences caused some of our dreams to shatter. We may have had a tendency to blame God for not answering our prayers. Based on the principles of the Program, our attitude toward prayer changes as we work the Steps. We learn to ask for God's will for us and to accept that He knows what is best. The old habit of praying for material things diminishes, and we replace it with prayers for guidance. We begin to rely on some of the slogans and prayers, such as "Let Go and Let God" or The Serenity Prayer. Our prayers can be as simple as "God, please help me," or "Thank you, God." Any prayer is helpful if it helps the individual. The only requirement for a prayer to be successful is that it be sincere, humble, and not for our own selfish gain.

Meditation is an ancient art that entails quieting the mind and not thinking. It is the channel through which we receive guidance from God. In order to meditate successfully, we must be willing to quiet our conscious mind and to remove the barriers of our conscious thoughts. This is difficult for some of us because we are unaccustomed to sitting still and relaxing. Meditation helps to calm us emotionally and to relax us physically. It helps us release energy we normally expend in keeping our emotions in high gear and our bodies taut.

An overview of the use of both prayer and meditation in a given day may be outlined as follows:

I. **BEGINNING OF THE DAY:**
   A. Review our plans for the day.
      1. Ask God to direct our thoughts and actions.
         a. To keep us free from self-pity, dishonesty, selfishness.
         b. To give us the guidance needed to take care of any problems.
      2. Ask God for freedom from self-will.
         a. To prevent our making requests unless others will be helped.
         b. To stop us from praying for our own selfish needs.

II. **DURING THE DAY, IN MOMENTS OF INDECISION OR FEAR:**

   A. Ask God for inspiration and guidance.
   B. Ask God for clear, intuitive answers.
   C. Reflect on Step Three and turn it over.
      1. Relax and breathe deeply several times.
      2. Be aware of any desire to struggle with a situation or person.
   D. Pray to God as often as necessary during the day.
      1. "God, please remove this _____." (feeling, obsession, addiction, etc.)
      2. "Thy will be done."
   E. If possible, call a support person simply to acknowledge what is happening.

III. **END OF THE DAY:**

A. Review the events of the day by practicing Step Ten and taking a personal inventory.
B. Take time to pray for knowledge of His will for us.
C. Acknowledge that this review is not intended to cause obsessive thinking, worry, remorse, or morbid reflection.
D. Pray to God, asking:
   1. For forgiveness.
   2. For guidance in corrective action we need to take.

The methods of prayer and meditation may vary; however, it is our intentions and the prayer content that matter. Our commitment is primarily to deepen our relationship and open our communication with God. This means being honest, sharing our innermost selves, confessing our wrong doings, and bringing our failings to Him for forgiveness. By our dedication to prayer and meditation, and by becoming aware of God's unconditional love and forgiveness, we are empowered to continue our life in awareness of His constant presence. If we continue to pray with patience and trust, the result can be only humility, love, and faith.

The importance of Step Eleven is that it tells us precisely the things to pray for. In this Step of spiritual awakening, we pray only for knowledge of His will for us and for the power to carry that out. The word "only" emphasizes the fact that from now on, we pray for nothing else except His will and the courage to go forward and do what He makes us want to do.

The miracle of this Step is that it changes our past method of praying into a form of meditation, whether we know how to meditate or not. Praying only for His will and for the power to carry that out drives all our personal concerns from our consciousness and allows us to concentrate only on His concerns. This very prayer empties our mind of our own wants and allows God to enter.

If we have thoroughly placed our will in His care and pray, we must trust that our will is being directed by Him. The power to carry that out will be the courage to do so, and He will also give us that.

Seeking guidance is a tricky matter because we are so accustomed to running our lives rigidly and making demands on God. Our own desires and opinions are so much a part of us that we are likely to view the will of a Higher Power in terms of our own feelings.

In Step Eleven, we concede complete willingness to accept God's will and whatever terms are offered. We are no longer in a position to demand anything, and the best we can hope for is relief from our agony. We stop making demands on our Higher Power and let things work out in a natural way.

Prayer and meditation are used to improve our conscious contact with God as we understand Him. If we are progressing satisfactorily with Step Eleven, there will be signs along the way. One sign is a deep sense of gratitude, accompanied by a feeling of belonging in the world at last. Another is our feeling of being worthy. We have a sense of being guided and sustained as we proceed with our activities.

It is not always easy to maintain this new way of life. We may face boredom and disillusionment after the early stages of inspiration and excitement. Step Eleven reminds us of the need to maintain the wonderful way of life we've been given. It is no quick fix. It is really Steps Two and Three practiced on a daily basis. It can be our guide for the rest of our lives. If we understand and follow it carefully, some of the changes in our lives will border on the miraculous. We can have continuous recovery along with the qualities we were seeking but never found.

Step Eleven does exact a price, and we must pay it if we expect favorable results. There is a price in giving up the self-will that led us into trouble. Part of the price is facing the need to become open-minded and being willing to change. Doing God's will can be as simple as accepting that there is no strain in doing God's will. As soon as we accept it as our own, we will experience complete peace and joy. Unless we experience this, we are refusing to acknowledge His will for us. And finally,

Step Eleven calls for faith and persistence—the very qualities that we applied so wrongly to our compulsive behavior.

4. Harry M. Tiebout, *The Ego Factors In Surrender in Alcoholism*, (New York: Journal of Studies on Alcohol, Inc.)
5. *Alcoholics Anonymous*. Third Edition, A.A. World Services, Inc (New York, NY), p.46.

STEP TWELVE

HAVING HAD A SPIRITUAL AWAKENING AS THE RESULT OF THESE STEPS, WE TRIED TO CARRY THIS MESSAGE TO OTHERS, AND TO PRACTICE THESE PRINCIPLES IN ALL OUR AFFAIRS.

The Twelfth Step is where we were headed when we started our journey toward recovery and a spiritual awakening. As we worked our way through the Steps, something inside told us that there was hope at the end of the journey. The mystery surrounding the Twelve Steps is that they really work for those who are willing to surrender to a Higher Power. A.A. tells us: "The joy of living is the theme of the Twelfth Step, and action is its key word."[6] If we have practiced the other eleven steps to the best of our ability, we will have a spiritual awakening.

The process of working the Steps can be likened to the transformation of a caterpillar to a butterfly. The caterpillar is not clear that it is going to be a butterfly. Everything that is part of its death and re-birth in the cocoon must be experienced. The story is told of a man who noticed a cocoon on a bush in his yard. As he started to pull it from the bush and throw it away, he noticed the end was opening and a butterfly was struggling to escape. In an effort to help the emerging butterfly, he took it inside and carefully cut the cocoon away with a razor blade. The butterfly feebly crawled from the open cocoon and, within a few hours, died. It needed the strength it would have gained from the struggle to free itself

79

in order to survive in the outside world. In a like manner, our working the Steps is something that only we can do. Any attempts to have another person do our work or find answers for us inhibits our own recovery and limits our ability to become strong.

Our spiritual awakening is a gift that places us in a new state of consciousness and being. It is usually accompanied by a complete change in values. Where there used to be darkness, we now begin to see light. For most of us, the awakening is subtle and can only be viewed with hindsight. The maturity we gain by working the Steps enables us to view many experiences, often painful, as being spiritual in nature. Our awakening can be viewed as the sum total of these individual experiences. With each of them, we can identify in some way or another how our Higher Power is guiding us.

We become able to do, feel, and believe things that are not possible by our own resources alone. We find in ourselves a degree of honesty, humility, peace of mind, and love that we had not previously possessed. Our new values are based on a realistic view of ourselves as children of God, and we recognize a need for emotional and spiritual balance in our lives. With the help of our Higher Power, we have discovered new abilities in ourselves we never knew existed.

It is important to remember that our spiritual awakening is an ongoing process. It may have begun early in the Steps, but it continues for the rest of our lives. It is not a distinct event with a clear beginning and ending. As our spiritual awakening continues, we become more lovable, make friends more easily, and feel more comfortable with people. Our relationships with our families improve as we draw closer, yet we recognize each other's independent identity. We no longer have unrealistic expectations of ourselves, and we accept ourselves for who we are.

Because we know this Program works and is working for us, we are ready to carry the message to others. This is the means by which the Program grows, prospers, and flourishes. We have healthy tools for reaching out to those people who are in bondage, as we once were. The message we carry is a liberating one. Sharing the message strengthens our own recovery and continues our spiritual growth. The gift we receive in return may be new strength or new insights. It is also a means of helping ourselves continue to grow emotionally. Whatever it may be, we can be assured of satisfaction from our desire to help another human being. The most effective way of convincing people of the value of the Steps is to be ourselves the way God created us. This alone will reflect examples of our miraculously transformed lives.

There is no formal qualification for working this Step, other than the willingness and the desire to tell our stories as honestly as we can. This is one time when being ourselves is the gift we give to others. This can happen anywhere when we are called upon to do volunteer work, share in meetings, or interact with co-workers and family members. As we share our story with others and help them to recognize their need, we are learning to be humble and to express ourselves honestly. When we carry the message, we share how the Twelve Steps have transformed our lives, taking time to share our miraculous experiences with others who are in need of help. We tell them what we used to be like, what happened to us as a result of the Steps, and what we are like now. As we share our experience, strength, and hope with newcomers, we help them find a way to solve their own problems, look at themselves honestly, and stop finding fault with others.

Working with newcomers can be a rewarding experience. These people are usually troubled, confused, and resentful. They are looking for "instant relief." They need guidance, and we can help them to understand that the Program represents pain and hard work. The rewards and miracles far outweigh the pain. We need to encourage the newcomers to be gentle with themselves and to take the Program one day at a time. This is also a growth experience for us as we reflect back on where we were when someone introduced us to the Program. When carrying the message, we must emphasize that the decision to join the Program is an individual one that is made by most of us when we have suffered enough, are tired of hurting, or in other words, when we have "hit bottom."

A recurring message throughout the Twelve Steps is the importance of humility and obedience to our Higher Power. As we diligently practice these principles in our daily affairs, the key factor for success is our relationship with our Higher

Power. Working closely with our Higher Power helps us stay on the right course by our considering Him as a source of guidance and support. We realize now that we cannot achieve peace in the world until we have achieved peace within ourselves. We cannot achieve peace and serenity within ourselves independently of a Higher Power. We must individually admit we are powerless and begin to work on our spiritual development, one day at a time, for the rest of our lives.

We can view our progress by comparing where we were with where we are now. Are we less isolated and no longer afraid of authority figures? Have we stopped seeking approval and become accepting of ourselves as we really are? Are we more selective of the people we choose to form relationships with, and are we able to keep our own identity while in a relationship? Have we developed the ability to express our feelings? Have our fears lessened? Have a lot of our character defects been transformed into assets, and are we behaving in a sane manner? If we are able to answer affirmatively to the above, we have come a long way since Step One when our character defects were active and damaging.

As we practice this new behavior in our daily affairs, life in general seems to start working better. For some of us, our examples in family and work environments have a positive effect on those around us, and we can see recovery in our loved ones. This is truly a measure of our progress and of our determination to change our lives and our behavior. The more committed we are to living the Steps on a daily basis, the more likely we are to have a continual spiritual awakening for the remainder of our lives.

A key factor in practicing the Steps in all our affairs is to become accustomed to "living" the Steps. If we are truly committed to working the Steps, we will see that most of our problems can be resolved through the Steps. The practice of taking a problem through all the Steps is very healing and can be done in a relatively short time. In doing this, we find support and guidance from our Higher Power. The end result usually provides an inner peace and an ability to deal directly with the problem.

We have no doubt found that the program really does work in all areas of our lives. All we need to do is be willing to try and to let go. We find that as our faith in our Higher Power increases, we become more willing to trust. As our trust grows, we become willing to turn over our lives more readily, and this furthers our spiritual development. The process is gradual, regenerative, and never-ending. We slowly become God-oriented and thus learn the meaning of love, growth, and serenity.

KEEP COMING BACK. IT WORKS.

TWELVE STEP REVIEW

Identify a situation or condition in your life that is currently a source of resentment, fear, sadness, or anger. It may involve relationships (family, work, or sexual), work environment, health, or self-esteem. Describe the situation and indicate your concern.

Use the following questions to apply the principles of the Twelve Steps to your situation.

STEP ONE: In what ways are you powerless, and how is this situation showing you the unmanageability of your life?

STEP TWO: How do you see your Higher Power as helping you to restore your sanity?

STEP THREE: How does being willing to turn your life over to the care of God assist you in dealing with this?

STEP FOUR: What character defects have surfaced? (e.g. fear of abandonment or authority figures, control, approval seeking, obsessive/compulsive behavior, rescuing, excessive responsibility, unexpressed feelings)

STEP FIVE: Admit your wrongs, at least to God and yourself.

STEP SIX: Are you entirely ready to have God remove the character defects that have surfaced?

STEP SEVEN: Can you humbly submit to God and ask Him to remove your shortcomings? If not, what is your resistance?

STEP EIGHT: Make a list of the persons being harmed.

STEP NINE: What amends are necessary, and how will you make the amends?

STEP TEN: Review the above Steps to be sure that nothing has been overlooked.

STEP ELEVEN: Take a moment for prayer or meditation, asking God for knowledge of His will for you.

STEP TWELVE: How can your understanding and spiritual awakening assist you in dealing with your problem?

APPENDIX ONE

SELF HELP RESOURCES

Adult Children of Alcoholics
Central Service Board
PO Box 35623
Los Angeles, CA 90035
(213) 464-4423

Al-Anon/Alateen Family Group Headquarters, Inc.
Madison Square Station
New York, New York 10010
(212) 683-1771

Alcoholics Anonymous World Services, Inc.
468 Park Avenue South
New York, New York 10016
(212) 686-1100

Debtors anonymous
P.O. Box 20322
New York, N.Y. 10025-9992

Emotions Anonymous
P.O. Box 4245
St. Paul, MN. 55104

Gamblers Anonymous
P.O. Box 17173
Los Angeles, CA 90017

Narcotics Anonymous
World Service Office
16155 Wyandotte Street
Van Nuys, CA 91406
(818) 780-3951

National Association for Children of Alcoholics
31706 Coast Highway, Suite 201
South Laguna, CA 92677
(714) 499-3889

National Clearinghouse for Alcohol Information
P.O. Box 1908
Rockville, Maryland 20850
(301) 468-2600

National Council on Alcoholism
12 West 21st Street
New York, New York 10010
(212) 206-6770

Overeaters Anonymous
World Service Office
2190 190th Street
Torrance, CA 90504
(213) 320-7941

APPENDIX TWO

SUGGESTED READING

Black, Claudia. *It Will Never Happen To Me.* Denver, CO: Medical Administration Company, 1982.

Cermak, Timmen. *A Primer on Adult Children of Alcoholics.* Pompano Beach, FL: Health Communications, Inc.

Friends in Recovery. *The Twelve Steps—A WAY OUT*, San Diego, CA: Recovery Publications.

Gravitz, H.L., and J.D. Bowden. *Guide to Recovery.* Holmes Beach, FL: Learning Publications, Inc.

Kritsberg, Wayne. *The Adult Children of Alcoholics Syndrome.* Pompano Beach, FL: Health Communications, Inc.

Schaef, Anne W. *Co-Dependence Misunderstood-Mistreated.* Minneapolis, MN: Winston Press, Inc.

Wegscheider-Cruse, Sharon. *Choicemaking.* Pompano Beach, FL: Health Communications, Inc.

Whitfield, Charles. *Healing The Child Within.* Pompano Beach, FL: Health Cmmunications, Inc.

Woititz, Janet. *Adult Children of Alcoholics.* Pompano Beach, FL: Health Communications, Inc.

APPENDIX THREE

THE TWELVE STEPS
OF
ALCOHOLICS ANONYMOUS

1. We admitted we were powerless over alcohol—that our lives had become unmanageable.

2. Came to believe that a Power greater than ourselves could restore us to sanity.

3. Made a decision to turn our will and our lives over to the care of God as we understood Him.

4. Made a searching and fearless moral inventory of ourselves.

5. Admitted to God, to ourselves, and to another human being the exact nature of our wrongs.

6. Were entirely ready to have God remove all these defects of character.

7. Humbly asked Him to remove our shortcomings.

8. Made a list of all persons we had harmed, and became willing to make amends to them all.

9. Made direct amends to such people wherever possible, except when to do so would injure them or others.

10 Continued to take personal inventory and when we were wrong promptly admitted it.

11. Sought through prayer and meditation to improve our conscious contact with God as we understood Him, praying only for knowledge of His will for us and the power to carry that out.

12. Having had a spiritual awakening as the result of these steps, we tried to carry this message to alcoholics, and to practice these principles in all our affairs.

Reprinted with permission of
ALCOHOLICS ANONYMOUS
WORLD SERVICES, INC.

APPENDIX FOUR

DAILY MEDITATION
JUST FOR TODAY

I will take a good look at myself and see that I have many addictive and compulsive traits that have become dominant in my life. I am at the mercy of these traits and unable to manage them. Seeing this, I admit that I need help.

I will acknowledge the presence of a Power greater than myself who has created me, is aware of all my needs, and is fully capable of healing me and restoring me to a condition of clarity and stability. This power is God as I choose to understand Him.

I will let go of the inclination to figure out my problems with my mind. No more analyzing . . . no more questioning. I now make a conscious decision to turn my life and my will over to the care and keeping of God. I surrender the thinking that tells me I must "run my own show" and make my own life happen. I am ready to be a TRANSFORMED (changed) person, beginning right now.

I will release the past, letting go of any guilt or regrets about what happened "back then." Finding fault or blaming myself and/or others keeps me stuck in the past.

I will forgive myself and others for the way we've been. I realize that our actions have risen out of fear and insecurity. I now allow myself and others to "be." I no longer pass judgment on our lives, our chosen paths, or our pattern of growth.

I will drop all anxiety about the future. I will live THIS DAY with as much joy, trust, and serenity as I can, realizing that this day is all I can handle.

I will let go of my tendencies to be dependent on persons, possessions, and patterns to fulfill me. I recognize that these things are only a temporary part of my existence and cannot provide the lasting security, inner peace, or true freedom that I yearn to experience on a daily basis.

I will take responsibility for all aspects of my life: my choices, my feelings, my physical and mental health, my spiritual well-being, my paths of growth, and the principles and values by which I live.

I will utilize all the energies within me that contribute to the betterment of my life and to the lives of others (e.g. expressing honesty, integrity, and kindness). To all else, I firmly say, "No, thank you."

I will thank God for the opportunity to be set free from old attitudes and behavior patterns that prevent me from moving in the direction of my needed healing.

I will willingly share with others the wisdom, peace, and strength I have received through this Program.

I will go forth into this day with enthusiasm, believing in my own value and worthiness, and with the determination to enjoy this day and give it my positive best, come what may.

Are you Ready for the Next Step in Recovery?

Start a writing Step Study using
The 12 Steps ... A Way Out

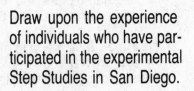

Draw upon the experience of individuals who have participated in the experimental Step Studies in San Diego.

Call or write:

Tools for Recovery
1201 Knoxville Street
San Diego, CA 92110
(619) 275-1350

SEE REVERSE SIDE

Writing Step Study Overview

Following is an outline of what to expect from participating in a Writing Step Study. Although the writing focuses on the book, **The 12 Steps — A Way Out,** it is important to include other reading material while you are working the Steps.

1. During the first three weeks, the meeting remains open so that anyone interested in finding out about the meeting format is welcomed to do so.

2. The meeting closes after the third week, at which time small family groups are formed. These groups are an important part of the Step Study process, and help to develop trusting, supportive relationships.

3. Beginning with the fourth week, the meeting is facilitated by each family group on a rotating basis. The meeting format is in the Appendix Two of the workbook.

4. Two weeks is spent on most of the steps.

5. It is recommended that you read the workbook material, and complete as much of the writing as is possible.

6. The weekly writing exercise, located in Appendix Three, is the central focus of the weekly meeting. Time is spent at the beginning of the meeting to complete the exercise, and is used as the basis for the family sharing.

7. It is important to keep in mind that you are doing this work for your own personal growth. Set your own pace and accept your progress without putting unrealistic expectations on yourself.

8. This program is worked **one day at a time.**

ORDER FORM

CODE	TITLE	QTY	UNIT PRICE	TOTAL
1058	It Will Never Happen To Me		$ 8.95	
1035	A Primer on Adult Children of Alcoholics		$ 3.00	
4901	The 12 Steps—A Way Out		$14.95	
4902	The 12 Steps for Adult Children		$ 6.95	
1057	Guide to Recovery!		$ 9.95	
1038	The Adult Children of Alcoholic Syndrome		$ 7.95	
1040	Co-Dependence Misunderstood-Mistreated		$ 7.95	
1033	Choicemaking		$ 9.95	
1029	Healing the Child Within		$ 8.95	
1034	Adult Children of Alcoholics		$ 6.95	
9001	The 12 Steps for Adult Children (4 cassette tapes)		$24.95	

Sub-Total

* Sales Tax

** Shipping & Handling

TOTAL

* 6% Sales Tax - CA Residents only
** Shpg. & Hand. Min. Charge — $1.75
    Orders over $25.00 — $3.00
    Orders over $50.00 —   6% of Total

Send this order form and a check or
money order for the total to:

TOOLS FOR RECOVERY
1201 Knoxville Street
San Diego, CA 92110

To order by phone, please call
(619) 275-1350

Visa and Mastercard Accepted

Bankcard # _____
Expiration Date _____
Signature _____
Allow 2-3 Weeks for Delivery - UPS

SHIP TO:

Name: _____
Address: _____
City, State: _____
Zip: _____ Phone: (___) _____

93